Only Trollops
Shave Above the Knee

The **Crazy, Brilliant,** and **Unforgettable**
Lessons We've Learned from Our Mothers

To Marilyn &
John

BLUE
—LOBSTER—
Book Co.

Table of Contents

For our mothers, our grandmothers, and all of the motherly womenfolk who have influenced our lives for the better. Even if it didn't seem so at the time, we were listening to you.

Introduction

When I was ten years old, I desperately wanted to shave my legs. Coming from strong European descent, I was (and still am) fair-skinned with rather hairy limbs. I didn't mind the few hairs that had suddenly sprouted on my knuckles, but the dark, ebony mass that had blossomed from my thighs down was shocking.

I'd grown self-conscious of the permeating *wool rug*, especially in the summers when I loved to wear bathing suits. So I did what any young girl would do: I asked my mother to shave.

"Absolutely not!" was her firm reply. I was simply too young, and *the earlier we women shave, the faster and more lush it grows back*, I was informed. I did not want thicker landscaping that grew at lightning speed. So I decided against shaving. Until I was thirteen.

After a horrifying experience at a neighborhood pool party, where my mammoth ways were placed under a microscope, I knew it was time to try again. It was time to approach the shaving subject with my mother for a second time. Surely she'd understand given the circumstances.

"Absolutely not!" was once again her firm reply.

"But, Mom! They were so mean! They were trying to pull the hairs out and calling me a boy!" I fired back, tears flowing down my face (which was thankfully hairless).

"You're not old enough to shave," she explained, and that was that.

Although I'd heard her words, I was not about to have my hairs plucked out one-by-one by my neighbors. I would take care of the situation.

I excused myself later that evening to take a bath. Inside the medicine cabinet, I found a pink bottle of Nair and several disposable razors. I thought about those "short shorts" and long legs the women sported on the liquid hair removal commercials. And then I read the instructions. The words *burning*, *accidental*, and *inflammation* immediately made me choose a razor over the Nair. Inflamed calves would've been a dead giveaway.

After soaking for ten minutes, I squirted five plump handfuls of shaving cream onto my legs and began shearing away, having no clue how to hold the razor or even which direction to go. There was no Internet to guide you back then, no Google or HelpMeMakeAPoorDecision.com, nor was my older sister still living at home. I was on my own.

Once I'd shaved the lower parts of my legs, I set my sights on the upper halves. There was hair up there too! Of course it had to be removed. I stood up to get the job done, managing to finish without even a nick. I emptied the bathtub, threw on my nightgown, and went to bed, relieved that I was now, for the most part, a hairless wonder.

The next morning as I sat at the table eating breakfast, my grandmother, whom we lived with, glanced down at the lower region of my body.

"Did you shave your legs?" she asked, an inquisitive, stern look crossing her face.

"I … I … Yes, I did. I had to because the kids were making fun of me." I made my case.

"Did you shave *all* of your leg?"

"Well, yes. Why?"

"There is absolutely no reason to shave your entire leg. Only trollops shave above the knee!" In this instance another word was used in place of "trollops."

"Grammie!" I was horrified. I had never heard her use that word in my entire life.

"It's true. Just shave the lower part of your leg." With that, she left the room.

After that day I was careful to not bring attention to my shaving habits. I continued to shear my entire legs, and still do, against my grandmother's warning and even though short shorts have never been my thing.

I've never fully understood why only trollops shave above the knee. But sometimes that's how it goes with motherly lessons, *right*? We're taught so many throughout our lifetime. Some are brilliant and filled with wisdom. Others are timeless. We carry those lessons with us and even pass them along to our children. Then there are those snippets of advice and teachings that leave us wondering what our mothers had been thinking. *Were they, too, dropped on their heads as children?* I guess we'll never know. All we can do is reap the advice that makes sense and ponder the advice that doesn't.

And that's how this book came to be. *Only Trollops Shave Above the Knee* is filled with the crazy, brilliant, and unforgettable lessons we've learned from our mothers—stories shared by more than forty word-crafty writers. Some of the tales will make you laugh; some will make you cry; and a few will leave you questioning how we ever survived our childhoods. Although they may at times seem a little faulty, *trust me*, our mothers (and motherly figures) could drive like Andretti, cook like Julia Child, and shake someone up like an Italian mobster. We've survived and thrived, and never forgotten their enlightening words.

Enjoy the book!

Crystal Ponti

Flying Butter Dishes

By Gabriella Brand

As I threw the butter dish across the room, my mother turned around just in time to see the beautiful blue porcelain shatter against the dining room wall. I don't remember aiming for her head, which was adorned with an elegant, tightly-wound hair bun, nor was I trying to hurt her. I just recall being very angry and upset. Seventh grade, with its social cliques and expectations, was the worst year of my life, and I took my frustrations out on my poor mother.

"I hate you," I screamed, the way I had seen people do in the movies.

She had told me that day that I couldn't wear black lipstick, the same kind all my friends were wearing.

"I hate you," I repeated, as if she hadn't heard me the first time.

"You are a monster!" she said, finally, biting her bottom lip. Then she began to cry. "You're not my daughter. You couldn't be my daughter," she said. "You are too disrespectful."

For a brief instant I wondered if she was right.

Maybe the hospital had made a mistake thirteen years before. Maybe some neglectful nurse had put me back in the wrong bassinet after a feeding. Maybe I really belonged to my best friend's mother, Mrs. McFarland, who was blissfully young, wore snappy, white tennis skirts, and drove a red convertible over the speed limit. My own mother, already gray-haired, usually wore conservative clothes and didn't even have a driver's license. She was old-school European, and fussy in ways that no other American mothers seemed to be.

"You're *ground up*," said my mother, snarling at me like a rabid dog.

"You mean grounded?" I said, with a sense of linguistic superiority. At least I could speak perfect English, even if I threw butter dishes.

"Yes. Grounded. That's it," she repeated. "You may not leave the house except to go to school."

I immediately called a friend, perhaps the McFarland girl with the cool mother, and began to complain vociferously.

"I can't go to the party on Saturday night. I'm grounded."

"Whadya do?" asked the friend.

"Lost my temper," I said, "again."

I basked in my friend's sympathy, until my mother overheard me.

"The phone is off-limits too," she announced. "Everything is off-limits until you behave like a decent human being."

That night she came up to my room on the pretext of drawing the shades. She sat on the edge of my bed, wedged up against the toy elephant that I had cherished since childhood.

She smoothed the bangs on my forehead with a cool hand and said goodnight, as if I were a little girl still needing to be tucked in, instead of a young adolescent with a chip on her shoulder.

"Your behavior," she began, "I detest it. I really do. But I still love you. Never forget that."

I don't remember if I told her that I loved her too. I probably turned my head away and gave her the silent treatment.

I was *that* kind of teenager.

The punishment only lasted a week or so. Not long enough for me to actually become respectful, that's for sure. I kept fighting with my mother, off and on, until the morning I left for college.

A full truce didn't come until I was almost twenty-five and pregnant with Child #1. My mother was the only person, besides my son's father, who was as happily obsessed with the baby as I was.

After he was born, she called frequently wanting to hear all about him.

"And he blows kisses, does he?" she'd ask. "He's so advanced!"

Even though we were living over a thousand miles apart, long before Skype or email, we managed to communicate frequently and well. She'd send me money for plane tickets to come home just for the pleasure of seeing me and my little guy. The child was docile and precious. I loved being his mother, and my mother enjoyed being his grandmother.

Child #2 was equally precious. But before long, he showed a very strong will and a mischievous spirit. He was only four when he threw his first "butter dish." It was a plastic bowl of oatmeal. After taking aim, he displayed the same fiery temper and lack of remorse as I once did.

It's not possible or practical to ground a four-year-old. He has no real social life.

I tried "time outs" and "Go to your rooms," and red stars and no stars, and all sorts of punishments. I tried bargains and badges and all the other stuff the parenting experts advised.

I was at my wit's end. A defiant child is a challenge at any age. And this one was not yet in kindergarten.

I confided to my mother about my frustration. She did get to witness my little monster's behavior for herself on occasion. No one forgot the day that Child #2, reaching the ripe old age of five, locked himself inside a rental car with the keys dangling in his hand and a big grin on his face. No amount of cajoling or threat could get him to open the doors.

"I'm going nuts! This kind of parenting isn't fun at all." I complained to my mother.

"I know what you mean," she said.

I don't think I really thought about my own horrible incident with the butter dish until a few weeks later when my mother sent me a little quotation handwritten on an index card.

"Children need love the most when they deserve it the least."

And there it was; the wisdom that my mother had been silently imparting for decades.

I knew immediately that she had experienced with me exactly what I was feeling with both my children. Exasperation, pure and simple. Complicated by feelings of inadequacy. *What kind of a pathetic mother am I?* Plus overdoses of all the other bad stuff: fear, guilt, anger, shame.

There were differences, of course. I hadn't really gotten on my mother's nerves until I was eleven or twelve. I had been a manageable, though impish, child. It was only as a pubescent that I became a complete brat. Selfish and nasty. Child #2 was never a brat. On the contrary, he was sweet and kind. But he was impossibly headstrong. He drove me crazy before he was out of diapers. Mercifully, he was quite well-behaved by the time he hit middle school.

My mother's little index-card saying became a mantra for me. Whenever my difficult child pulled and tugged his way to glorious independence, causing me to tear out my hair, I just kept trying to give him one message, the same one my mother had tried to give me. *I love you.* Not your behavior. *But you.* Always. And forever. Even when it is hard for me to feel much of anything. Even when you don't deserve much of anything. I love you, unconditionally.

Is there a more important lesson that a mother can give?

Gabriella Brand's short stories, essays, and poetry have appeared in *The Christian Science Monitor, Room Magazine, Culinate, The Mom Egg, The Binnacle, Three Element Review,* and elsewhere. One of her short stories was nominated for a Pushcart Prize in 2013. She lives mostly in New England, where she teaches several foreign languages and travels widely, mostly on foot, around the globe. Her family is a never-ending source of inspiration, both literary and otherwise.

The Kid Collector

By C. Lee Reed

Remember when you were a little kid and you genuinely felt wronged by the people that birthed you, so you swore that you'd never become your mother?

This proclamation usually coincided with the exact moment that you were found guilty of some misbehavior: skipping school, lying, or teasing your sister. Your tirade would include foot stomping, grumbling, and the occasional raised finger behind a back. You would hole up in your bedroom and wonder, "Why can't Mom understand how I feel? How dare she treat me, her favorite, this way? I'll never do that to my own kids."

Of all the atrocities in the free world, nothing sparks more fear in kids than turning into our parents. Please don't get me wrong. I have always been very close with my mother; but every woman alive has prayed, at some point in her life, to never end up just like her.

As a parent with over eighteen years of experience under my ever-widening belt, I can happily use hindsight to relive so many of my childhood moments. I often think back to times in my youth and recall what I thought I'd do then and how that thought actually differs than my current reality. For the most part, I have handled my daughter's infractions exactly as my mother did. The truth is, I rarely would have changed anything about how my parents handled raising me.

Like every young girl, ignorant of heredity's strong ties, I fought long and hard to be different than my mom. That's hard to do when you are the spitting image of the woman who gave you life. My entire adolescence was dedicated to avoiding the obvious traits that are probably the most defining part of my being. Caring, nurturing, and coddling just come naturally, as they did for her. I now understand her need to love others beyond our immediate walls.

Most importantly, I can now proudly embrace the fact and exclaim that *I am my mother's daughter!* Not just a little, but certifiably 110 percent hers. I have learned to become my mother. Exactly like my mother. Thankfully those prayers—sent so many years ago from my twin-sized bed—went unanswered.

Growing up, my mom was *the mom* that every kid wanted. She was the *fun mom*, the *cool mom*, our *room mom*—the one who brought us homemade cupcakes each holiday and the *Girl Scout leader mom*. She cheered my friends and me on at our events, memorized the words to every chorus song, took us shopping on the weekends, and let us play in her car for hours on end. *Is there really anything better than sitting in your 1979 station wagon, with the radio blaring, singing in the driveway?*

Without even realizing it or trying hard, my mother inevitably became the *"wish she was my mom"* mom.

My mother collected children. Wherever she went, they instantly became family. Recreation parks, churches, and schools were never off limits and supplied her with a steady fix. My mom had an open-door policy and they reveled in it. Every person was welcome; all were invited and encouraged to apply. Holiday celebrations were shared with whichever kid needed it most. Boo-boos were nursed back to health promptly. There was always someone to help and take care of. I told myself that as an adult, "My child will always come first."

Puberty sent several of us into rough patches. Mom's kid collection grew to include several "orphans." Kids who had no place else to go were suddenly hanging out at our home. Troubled children, as defined by some invisible judge my mom never met, were suddenly front and center at our dinner table. Those with moms who had given up were placed in the carpool, lest they attempt to get out of line again. No matter how big the gang grew, Mom was always available to listen to our tall tales, laugh at our jokes, or chauffeur our little non-driving butts around. Advice was spoken freely and honestly. Money switched hands more openly than the stock exchange. Guidance was ever present; although, as a working mother, I had no idea how she did it. Maybe she really did have eyes in the back of her head. I cannot remember even one meltdown. Ever!

As a teen it was often hard to understand why I wasn't enough. I was her first born after all. Not that for even a minute I'd ever felt neglected. It was just pure jealousy. She was and is MY mom. Her kid collection wanted in on it, and she was always there for them. Yes, she was there for me, too, but I'd earned the right to use that precious MOM title and loved her like no other. I didn't want to share. No worries, I told myself. When I have kids, "I will never do that."

Years later, I have found myself in the exact same scenario with my own daughter. So many of her friends have meandered in and out of my grasp that I've lost count. Some tiptoed lightly across my path, and a few snowplowed their way into a special pocket of my soul, to remain permanently. I now fully appreciate and understand the lesson my mother taught me about parenting. I feel an overwhelming desire to love the children who are part of our lives. My daughter's schoolmates were kids by proxy. Her boyfriends became the sons I'd never have. Pool party attendees were doted on. Neighbors provided for. Children without a parent on field trips instantly became part of my buddy system. I know the names of their siblings, their favorite meals, and their secret dreams to play in a rock band. *Now, where did I learn that from?*

Sadly my parenting is coming to a close, as least in the hands-on everyday way. I weep over the graduation of my own brood. Not the literal cap and gown event; the growing up and leaving the nest and not needing me anymore variety. I have watched tons of them grow, dragged them through theme parks, taught them to drive, studied with them for mid-terms, cried with them over broken friendships, fed them, and collected every one of them inside my heart. Just like my mother did back in the day when I swore, "I would never be like her."

In case you're wondering, and I know you are, my mom is still an avid collector. What once were toddlers and teens, is now the elderly and occasional stray dog. She has welcomed a generation of grandchildren and their friends into her open arms, yet still treats me like her most precious gift. I hope I have done her subtle lessons justice.

She taught me that love is unlimited, unending, and meant to be shared with those that surround you. And letting go, when the time is right, means you'll have more room for the next.

Now, where did I put that kid?

C. Lee Reed, from *Helicopter Mom and Just Plane Dad*, is one-half of a parenting team that hopes to change the world's perception of helicopter parenting by proving that no harm comes to children whose parents hover. You can stay highly involved in your children's lives and still maintain a happy, healthy, and loving connection. She is a contributing author to *The Mother of All Meltdowns*, a collection of funny and heartwarming stories to help mothers cope with the not-so-dark side of parenting.

Nothing Ventured, Nothing Gained—
Except an Outrageous Phone Bill

By Crystal Ponti

"YOUR PHONE BILL IS HOW MUCH? WERE YOU CALLING FROM THE RITZ? IS DONALD TRUMP PICKING UP THE TAB?"

I'll never forget my mother's words echoing through the lines as I attempted to explain (justify?) the outrageous phone bill I'd racked up in only a month. What might've been a normal bill for a small call center was preposterous for a residential account like mine. I had single-handedly accumulated sixteen hundred dollars in charges from Pine Tree Telephone. As a company that had recently been party lines only, I imagine they struck gold that day. The party was definitely over for me, but just beginning for them—blow horns and all. I was the piñata.

Thankfully, I have my mother. If there is one person that I have always been able to count on, it's her. Though thick and thin, she has stood by me as I've done some pretty stupid and reckless stuff. This includes the phone bill catastrophe that happened while attempting to start a business and raising two babies.

The day the bill arrived I'd contemplated giving up and rejoining the work force. She reassured me that nothing ventured meant nothing gained—yeah, yeah, yeah. I'd heard it all before. After a wretched ugly cry in the throes of her lap, I left her house to fetch the mail.

I was immediately distracted by a Fingerhut package containing *Teenage Mutant Ninja Turtle* curtains. I'd saved up just enough money and could finally finish the boys' room in half-shell, hero style. The second I arrived back home I threw the stack of bills onto the counter and kicked into Martha Stewart-mode. The first step was a fresh coat of blue paint.

After a few hours of painting and very much looking like Smurfette, I ventured into the kitchen for a cup of coffee. As I waited for it to brew, I shuffled through the bills. Electric bill—check. Quarterly tax bill—check. Telephone bill—che—

"WHAT?" I screamed.

It shouted back, "SIXTEEN HUNDRED DOLLARS!"

If I had to pinpoint the exact moment I first noticed an issue with anxiety this would be it. My insides knotted up like a strand of Christmas lights, and sweat peeped through my pores.

Holy shit. *What did I do?*

I was barely bringing in enough money to pay the normal phone bill, let alone one that could supply service to a neighborhood of gossiping seniors.

Complicating matters was the bill had been totally revamped. The previous month it was easy to read. This time it was as if Good Will Hunting had crafted some mathematical formula on several sheets of blazing white paper. The bill was broken down into all sorts of line items, but one suddenly stood out: AOL dial-up, one gazillion minutes! It flashed like a sign in front of a strip club.

Back in the day, the Internet wasn't a flat monthly fee. You typically tried for an available FREE line and when you couldn't get one (which was always), you paid by the minute. I happened to have AOL installed on my new desktop. And had turned into a fiend for those three magical words: *You have mail!*

But that didn't mean I was totally irresponsible. I normally logged on to the paid line just for a moment or two, when necessary, to check email and respond to messages. That was until I discovered a chat room for Mainers. Now here was an easy networking opportunity, so I thought. I wouldn't have to leave home, and I could promote my business to those who might be interested. It was a win-win! *So. I. Thought.*

As any busy work-from-home parent knows, things get a little chaotic when you attempt to balance work-life with the constant demands of little people. Sometimes you forget to do something and sometimes you get interrupted in the middle of an important task—like logging off a paid line so you won't continuously use it for days on end thinking you had hit the holy grail of endless free Internet. Oh, yes, I did. For days. And countless minutes.

When I realized what I'd done, I immediately called my mother.

"YOUR PHONE BILL IS HOW MUCH? WERE YOU CALLING FROM THE RITZ? IS DONALD TRUMP PICKING UP THE TAB?"

I'm pretty sure that everyone within five-square-mile radius heard her.

"It was an accident. I must have been distracted by the kids and completely forgot to log off the paid line."

"Paid line? Like an 800-number?"

"What?"

"What paid line? Were you calling one of those tele-psychics?"

"No, Mom. The Internet. I couldn't get a free line, so I logged on to Pine Tree Telephone and forgot to log off."

"The what? Who were you calling, and why were you on the phone for so long?"

"Oh, my god, Mom. The INTERNET! I was on AOL checking my email and networking for the business."

"You were networking? Well that's good. But I don't understand why you just didn't do it in person and why the bill would be so much for a few phone calls."

My mother came from an era when cars still had to be cranked when started and black-and-white TVs were really cool. She was unable to grasp my technology dilemma.

"Mom, you know how I bought a computer to use for work? With the computer I am able to log onto a service that allows me to talk to a bunch of people all at once, rather than having to leave home or meet in person. It's done using a service called America Online. Sometimes you can get a free line, and there are no phone charges. Other times you have to log on using your telephone provider, which isn't free. I made the mistake of logging on using Pine Tree Telephone and forgot to log off

18

... for days. So now I have this huge phone bill that I can't pay. Basically, I'm screwed."

"I see." She said in a calm, relaxed voice. "I think you should just call the telephone company, and tell them that you made a mistake."

"I highly doubt they are going to erase the charges because a dumb ass forgot to click a button."

"Nothing ventured, nothing gained. Right?"

"I just can't do it, Mom. That almost seems like begging. And I'm so embarrassed."

After we hung up, I sulked in a corner trying to figure out what to do. I would surely lose phone service altogether in thirty days, because I could not come up with that kind of money and feed the kids too. My pride also took over, yielding me an even bigger dumb ass. I had dug myself into a hole without even knowing I had a shovel. The phone suddenly ringing brought me back to Internet hell on earth.

"Hello?"

"I called Pine Tree Telephone on your behalf," my mother said ever so matter-of-factly.

"You did WHAT?" I was nearly freaking out.

"They agreed to remove all but five hundred dollars of the charges. I told them that I would pay the rest. You just need to pay me back when you can."

"How did you get them to agree? They have a monopoly on phone service."

"I picked up the phone and called. Then I asked nicely. They were happy to help. Sometimes you just have to swallow your pride and try. Nothing ventured, nothing gained. You can throw Donald's number away now."

In that moment I was taught one of the greatest life lessons. Sometimes we have to step outside of our comfort zones to achieve what seems impossible. Nothing is a sure thing, but if you don't try, you'll simply never know.

Although the business endeavor didn't work out, I would later land a great job with an online company that seemed totally out of reach. I was brave and ventured. And I gained considerably.

As far as my mother, she continues to be my biggest cheerleader. Even if we don't speak the same language all of the time.

No, Ma. I don't work for "the Google."

Crystal Ponti is the founder of Blue Lobster Book Co., a self-publishing boutique. Prior to launching her own business she worked for and advised some of the largest sites in the world and spent a number of years as a business and marketing planning consultant. She recently served as Managing Editor, Contributing Author, and publisher of the books *The Mother of All Meltdowns and Clash of the Couples*. She blogs at *MommiFried*, an outlet for her creative writing and a way for her to share her later-in-motherhood experiences with all women and parents. She is a Hall of Fame writer for *Scary Mommy*, and a regular contributor to Felicity Huffman's site *What The Flicka?*, *Business2Community*, and *The Huffington Post*. When she is not busy consulting, blogging, or writing, she can be found nurturing a beautiful family of five children, a wonderfully Italian husband, and an African-gray parrot with a colorful vocabulary.

Mama Hankered for Hankies

By Terri Elders

When I dropped into a local shoe store the other day, I spied a display of replica vintage ladies hankies, each tidily encased in a plastic envelope. I'd scurried through my errands that afternoon, but now I relaxed. I even stopped checking my wristwatch as I shuffled through the attractive assortment.

Time reversed itself, and once again I became that adolescent girl back in the early 1950s, searching for a perfect gift for Mama. I'd sure be stymied, forced to choose among these flower and forest-themed hankies. I sorted through squares of roses, orchids, daisies, violets, mums, lily of the valley, daffodils, tulips, and even leaves.

If Mama were still alive, I'd send this one to her for Mother's Day, I mused, admiring a particularly fetching pink and red rosebud hankie. I wondered if I could think of someone else who might be pleased to receive it as an unexpected gift in the mail, tucked inside a greeting card.

I closed my eyes, remembering how Mama always hankered for hankies. Then I blinked them open, as an odd thought struck me—*or did she?* There's no doubt that she always had a fresh handkerchief or two tucked into her purse and nearly a whole shoe box full in her bedroom closet. She carried them with her always, even after Kleenex came about and was marketed as a substitute for hankies.

"Why should I throw good money in the waste basket?" Mama once sniffed during an early 1950s shopping trek through Piggly Wiggly, when I suggested we pick up some Kleenex. She scowled at me and even seemed to repress a shudder. "It doesn't cost a cent more for me to wash out my hankies." You'd have thought I'd suggested she trade in her signature high-heeled pumps for a pair of the popular new rubber flip flops! "Besides, ladies carry handkerchiefs. Going somewhere without one would be like going to a church without white gloves!"

I wonder if Mama really had been all that fond of her little hemmed snippets of cotton cloth. Or could it really have been a fear of Daddy's disapproval of anything he deemed extravagant? I can still remember him growling with displeasure one steamy June afternoon, in those days before air conditioning.

"It's too hot this week to bake a cake," Mama announced, swiping her forehead with a favorite mint green embroidery-edged hanky. "I want to go to the store to get a cake for the girls' party this weekend." My sister and I, with birthdays five days apart, always celebrated together. Daddy's frown vanished when Mama elaborated, "Wonder Bread's day-old bakery might have something suitable."

I still recollect Mama's pleasure in being able to add a magazine to her purchases at the checkout counter the day after payday. She and her neighbors swapped and swapped again their favorite housekeeping and movie magazines, and even an occasional *True Romance,* which I seem to remember they'd hide from their husbands and younger children.

The Great Depression, and subsequent rationing during World War II, had taught this generation the value of frugality. When I was growing up I frequently heard, "Use it all. Wear it out. Make it do or do without." The war years' slogan had certainly become my parents' joint mantra.

Then again, Mama might have considered that in those days, when handkerchiefs were still relatively inexpensive, they'd be something affordable for a youngster like me, who made her spending money for Christmas and birthdays gifts through babysitting and waitressing at Owl Drug Store's lunch counter. Because no matter what the occasion—even after I became an adult and could afford more elaborate gifts—Mama always claimed that's what she wanted.

"Just get me a card and a hankie," she'd say, with a sweet smile. I don't know why I continued to ask, already knowing how she'd answer.

In later years I began to purchase other gifts, mostly her favorite cologne, Emeraude. But I still tucked a hankie into her cards. I remember the last one I bought for her. It was in 1983, and it had been my first trip to Paris. I'd found a D. Porthault hankie embroidered with the Eiffel Tower.

"Just what I wanted," she exclaimed, eyes lighting up. "How did you ever guess?"

Because it was *always* what she wanted. Or at least claimed to. And maybe it was. Maybe those hard decades of her early adulthood had shaped her to be satisfied with simple delights and pleasures, an occasional treat from a day-old bakery, a *Woman's Day* at the checkout, or a square of freshly laundered embellished cloth to tuck into her pocket or purse.

A year ago, in Paris once again, I'd lingered at the handkerchief counter at Galleries Lafayette. I wished I could have presented Mama with another frilly feminine square embroidered with the Eiffel Tower. I'd bought one for myself, anyway.

Now in the shoe store, a sales clerk interrupted my reverie. "May I help you?"

"I'll take this one," I answered, settling on the pink and red rosebuds.

Mother's Day was coming up fast, I thought, as I drove home. Not long ago, my friend, Ruthie, had lost her mom; her mother, in her late nineties, had been born just a few years after mine. Ruthie once confided that her mom shared my mother's professed love of handkerchiefs.

Though she'd expected it for years, the death hit her hard. Ruthie had even posted on Facebook that she'd never really realized what grief felt like until her mother's funeral. I remembered the New Year's Day when I'd learned that my own mom had finally died, after years of decline with Alzheimer's. I'd felt as if the bottom had dropped out of my world.

When I got home, I tucked the hanky into a "thinking of you" card for Ruthie, and added a few words. *Sending this in memory of our moms as Mother's Day approaches*, I wrote. I hoped it might offer her some comfort when Mother's Day actually arrived.

A few days later my phone rang. It was Ruthie.

"What a wonderful surprise ... and how it took me back in time," she chirped. "I felt like a girl again, sprinkling that hanky with my favorite cologne. And I could hear my mother's voice reminding me that ladies always carried handkerchiefs."

I'm planning another trip to the shoe store soon. I have other friends who might want to recall on Mother's Day the simple things their mothers loved and their way of inspiring us to appreciate those delightful things as well.

Terri Elders recently returned to her Southern California roots after a decades-long odyssey. Her creative nonfiction has appeared in over a hundred anthologies. She is co-editor of *Not Your Mother's Book...* *On Travel.*

Damn Girl, What Did You Do to Your Eyebrows?

By Carrie Groves

To honor the milestone that was my thirteenth birthday, my mother took my face in her hands, looked soulfully into my eyes, and said, "Baby, you need to pluck your eyebrows."

And I'll be damned if she wasn't right.

No matter what lies my parents might tell you, I was not a raving beauty when I was growing up. I don't even think I would put the word "beauty" in there. Maybe "raving" would fit, because I've always had a flair for the dramatic—but that's it. A better description would be: *a skinny, pale, bookworm who wore glasses and sported an especially kinky Toni home perm.*

As I got closer to my teen years and became keenly aware of my awkwardness, I tried to improve my appearance in any way I could. Armed with a Caboodle filled with pastel-colored makeup, Aqua Net for mile-high bangs, and enough Electric

Youth perfume to form a Pigpen-style cloud around my head, I thought I was well on the road to averageness.

There was just one thing holding me back: my glasses. They were sad, plastic, and the lenses were thicker than the milkshakes that never brought a boy to my backyard. So, the summer I turned thirteen, I stopped wearing them.

This was not the smartest decision because I was living in Chicago at the time and regularly walked up and down busy streets. When you can't find your glasses without your glasses, there's a good chance you won't see a passing bus when you're not wearing them, so you're more than likely to become a road pancake.

In the interest of keeping me alive, and not to pander to my vanity, my mom allowed me to get contact lenses for my birthday. The heavens opened, their golden rays fell upon my face, and a choir of angels celebrated this triumph. *Hallelujah!*

To this day, it is the greatest gift I have ever received.

On the sainted day, I entered LensCrafters with all of the self-importance a thirteen-year-old could possess. Regally, I sat down, popped in my new lenses, took them out, and put them back in all in record time. I was bound and determined to wear them and wear them well.

I think the two years I had already spent carefully layering on mascara and eye shadow, so it showed through my coke bottle lenses, had toughened up my eyes to the point where I could easily poke them to make the magic happen. Thank you, Cover Girl.

Now that I no longer wore glasses, it was apparent to my mother that I needed to make a few changes, starting with the bushy eyebrows that had been hiding behind my massive frames.

At the time, I thought she was being a little too blunt. Aren't parents supposed to think their children are always beautiful, even if they have small furry creatures above their eyes? But I now know that's not what she meant. She loved me enough to intervene before my eyebrows engulfed my face.

It's like when someone has food in their teeth or their zipper is down. It's embarrassing for everyone when you tell them, but the other person needs to know.

I also like to think that on a deeper level she was teaching me that in times of change you need to take a close look at yourself and your environment and see if anything else needs to change to keep up with the improvements. Or maybe she really was concerned that I would go through life resembling a female version of Abe Vigoda.

Ever the teacher, she kindly introduced me to my first pair of tweezers. She explained that you needed to grasp the offending hair and swiftly pull up and out to get rid of it. Demonstrating on her own eyebrows, she made it look easy.

Little did I know the torture that awaited me.

I took the tweezers, and instead of grabbing the errant hair, I stabbed myself in the eyelid. On the second attempt I managed to seize the hair and pull.

Oh. My. Sweet. Baby. Jesus.

My eyebrow throbbed with pain, and tears raced forward to try and soothe the brushfire forming above my eye. To add insult to injury, I hadn't removed the hair. It was stubbornly clinging to my brow bone.

Fueled by indignant rage, I rounded on my facial caterpillars and decimated them. When I looked in the mirror and saw perfectly groomed brows, I felt victorious. And, let me say, victory feels pretty damn good.

Then came the second lesson from my mother: How to Soothe Angry, Pink Eyelids.

Two cucumber slices and a cup of tea later, my mom decided I was strong enough to handle a second revelation about my appearance: my makeup routine needed an overhaul.

The same makeup that made my eyes pop behind my plastic frames and made me strong enough to withstand putting contact lenses in, also made me look like a mini Tammy Faye Bakker with my glasses off.

Subtlety has never been my forte, so I had a hard time with the lesson in moderation my mother tried to teach me. And, frankly, I was unable to fully understand this for many years. I still feel chagrined by the amount of liquid eyeliner I used during high school.

Now that I have kids of my own, I hope that I will be able to guide them during times of change the way my mother helped me. At the very least, I have a feeling she'll be able to help me find a good pair of tweezers.

Carrie Groves is the author of the blog, *Ponies and Martinis*. When she is not trying to keep her kids and dogs in line, she enjoys wine, writing, and song. Carrie is a regular contributor to *BLUNTmoms* and has been featured on *Mamapedia* and *Mamalode*.

You Won't Get Pregnant if You Use an Aspirin

By Jill Robbins

"Mom, I wanna talk about getting on the pill."

I said *this* to my mother, full of the sort of confident swagger that only a fourteen-year-old with second base firmly in her sights could possess.

"The pill, huh?" My mom was outwardly calm, cool, and collected, although I thought I noticed a little twitch in the vein at her temple. Now that I've survived the battle years—er, I mean the teen years—with my own daughter, I imagine this might have been the part where my mother regretted telling me stuff like, "Well of course you can talk to me about anything, honey."

"That's right." I nodded eagerly, anticipating a poignant mother-daughter bonding moment followed by scheduling a trip to the gynecologist's office where I'd emerge with the cool, round plastic packet of magical little pills that would enable me to go all the way with Rodney Miller without the fear of teen pregnancy spoiling my fun and romance. Two girls in my freshman class had already gotten "in trouble." I was doing the responsible thing by talking to my mom about taking steps to prevent pregnancy. All my friends were "doing it," or they were at least on the pill as a proactive measure. This was the early eighties and *safe sex* only meant not getting knocked up. *Doesn't that make you long for simpler times?*

My mom had indeed told me I could talk to her about anything, so I fully expected my announcement that I wanted to jump on the birth control bandwagon would be met with acceptance. Perhaps an awkward, "Oh my little girl's becoming a woman," mushy kind of moment. After all, my mom knew my feelings for Rodney Miller, who was the center of my teenage universe and most assuredly her future son-in-law. He also had the misfortune of being nicknamed "turkey neck" by my dad, but I loved him madly despite of this, because, as every fourteen-year-old knows, first love *always* lasts forever. This was before tattoos were commonplace, but I'd written *Jill + Rodney 4Ever* on my Trapper Keeper—in pen. This was true love, I tell ya.

"I'll tell you about the only pill you need," my mom began, the little vein in her forehead becoming just a little more prominent. "You just need to get yourself an aspirin."

Aspirin? I was all ears thinking I was about to enter the inner sanctum of womanly secrets. My friends and I had been whispering about the magical properties of the birth control pill in washrooms and at slumber parties for years, and here I was about to discover that aspirin did the trick just as well. So I thought. I leaned forward, as one does when they're about to receive an important message.

My mom's expression was very serious as her eyes scanned my face. I was certain she was taking a reflective moment to gauge the level of maturity in my eyes to make extra sure I was really ready to learn the secrets of womanhood.

"You take one aspirin," she began dramatically, "and place it on the side of your knee." She paused, making sure I was paying close attention. I was. I was confused, but I was soaking it all in. "You pull your other knee in, and hold the aspirin in place. Don't let it go. As long as you're holding that aspirin between your knees, you can't get pregnant."

It took a minute to fully process her words.

If you want to inject logic, the laws of physics, and acrobatics into the equation, you probably actually *can* get pregnant while holding an aspirin between your knees, although I doubt it would be any fun. The message from my mom was loud and clear: keep your legs shut.

Modern moms and daughters might argue that this is an unrealistic response. Kids are going to have sex and have sex much earlier than parents would like them to have sex, right? Might as well be proactive and make sure they're protected against unwanted pregnancies or, worse yet, all the things you can catch nowadays that we'd never heard of back when I was an eager and hormonal teenager.

But the conversation didn't end there. What followed was "part two" of the awkward birds and bees talk that we'd had before I hit puberty. *This* talk didn't involve a picture book titled *All About Your Body* that had a smiling, awkward-looking girl wearing a macramé vest on the cover. We didn't use technical terms like "pituitary" or "nocturnal emissions." And this is what I learned from my mom about men and women:

1. If a boy won't ring the doorbell or look your parents in the eye, you should think about moving on.
2. Always have a twenty dollar bill hidden in your wallet for cab fare. If you ever want to come home early, you won't have to rely on someone else to get you there. (*I realize twenty bucks might not get you very far these days, but it's still good advice.*)
3. You will make mistakes and poor choices when it comes to men, and that's okay. When it happens, learn from your mistake, hold your head up high, and march forward like you mean it.
4. Just because you say "yes" once doesn't mean the answer always has to be yes. Give yourself permission to change your mind. You don't owe anyone anything. Repeat, you don't owe anyone anything.
5. A boy won't die if he doesn't have sex. Really, he won't.
6. You don't have to tell anyone your secrets. Know when to share and when to keep something to yourself. You can't take it back once it's out there.
7. Nobody can make you feel anything except for you. You're in charge of your own emotions. If a man makes you unhappy, it's because you allowed him to do it.
8. Your virginity doesn't define you. You're not more womanly because you chose to have sex, and you're not less virtuous because you lose it. That said, you can only give it away once. Choose wisely.
9. During this conversation my mom never actually told me to wait until I was married to have sex. She never told me that fourteen was too young to make that kind of decision (it is). She didn't tell me that nice girls don't, although maybe that was implied with the aspirin trick.

We ended the conversation without any mention of a doctor's appointment for me. Although I was vaguely disappointed, I realized later that it was more because I wouldn't have that cool pack of little white pills in my purse to show all my girlfriends—to be part of a world that supposedly knew the secrets of womanhood. That day I learned there was more to being a woman than I'd realized, and that maybe, just maybe, I needed to keep the training wheels on for a little bit longer.

We don't use aspirin for aches and pains that much these days, but every time I see it on a store shelf or in someone's bathroom, I think of the important stuff I've learned from my mom and marvel at how long her advice has stuck with me, because fourteen was exactly a long frickin' time ago. I can fit fourteen into the age I am now exactly three times.

I never did have sex with turkey-neck Rodney Miller. I did, however, have to convince my mom to buy me a new Trapper Keeper before the end of the school year, because as it turns out, it wasn't *love 4Ever* after all.

Jill Robbins is a wannabe wine snob and sometime runner from San Antonio, Texas. She has a degree in Social Psychology which has so far not helped at all with understanding the behavior of her husband and three children. She writes about adoption, motherhood, and midlife on her blog, *Ripped Jeans and Bifocals*. She is a regular contributor to *The Huffington Post*, *Babble*, *Mamalode*, and *BLUNTmoms*. She's been published on *The Washington Post* and is a 2015 cast member of Listen to Your Mother, Austin. She someday hopes to write the books that are living in her head.

Sauce with a Side of Grace

By Angila Peters

My momma taught me more than just good manners, proper hygiene, and how to curl your eyelashes. She gave me something much more valuable: balls.

Yes, when my Rubbermaid totes were packed, and I was driven to a college dorm room, I knew how to call out the bull and stick it back in its pen—or, basically, how to deal with other people's crap.

I grew up watching her every move like most little girls do. Of course, I mastered the art of folding underwear and cleaning a house minutes before company arrives. But subconsciously, through her actions and relationships with others, I witnessed the fine art of sticking it to those who were nasty.

She dealt with rude customer service by tapping her fingers loudly on counter tops or stretching her gum out far and slowly chewing it back up; all the while balancing a womanly stature with her inner brat who was fighting to be seen.

Yes, as a child I was embarrassed by some of her one-woman shows of disgruntlement. But I was storing away memories of her tiny victories for future use.

I learned from an early age that sticks and stones could break my bones, but words were meant to be thrown back sarcastically, processed privately, and dusted off eloquently.

Most moms have gum in their purses. Mine had her collection of next moves and comebacks. The rebuttals were not necessarily mean. They were delicately saucy with enough grace to still be called a lady—just one who tosses her hair, raises an eyebrow, and butts a cigarette out on your shoe. (*It was the seventies. All moms smoked!*)

My mother was the original Sweet Brown. "Ain't nobody got time fo' that," was her response when the unreasonable, ridiculous, and rude surfaced.

She always knew how to deal with the jerks and how to sniff them out. And no one was safe when she detected a dickhead move. My sixth grade teacher found that out the hard way.

When I was given an assignment to write a speech about optimism, my mom navigated me through writer's block. What we came up with was a unique twist and a rather original topic. It was not what the other kids were doing, as I was taking a risk and a step toward being unique.

I wrote and then read it in front of my class. I was chosen to go on to the city finals.

When my teacher called to tell my parents he didn't think my speech should have made it past his classroom, he didn't know who he was dealing with. This teacher was one of those classy "pick on a few weak ones" and "toughen 'em up" kind of guy.

My momma had some advice for him, "Shove it." But of course in much nicer words, "Well, we will see you at the finals."

I knew he didn't believe in me and that rocked my confidence. So with the courage mom forced me to find, I stood up in front of an audience of strangers and tried not to barf. I was competing against high school kids, classmates, and my teacher's disagreement. He sat in the front row as a constant reminder.

I nailed the speech, placing third overall—right there, in that room. My parents were beyond proud, but a lot of their cheerfulness clearly held some "In your face, sucka!" attitude that I was too young to deliver.

There was possibly more sauce than grace that night, but it taught me not to change my path because someone said I wasn't good enough.

There were other lessons taught as well.

I was sixteen when my parents left me in charge of the house for a weekend. As soon as they were out the door, I did the obvious. Yes, I planned a small party.

My intimate gathering, however, turned into something much more when the invite went viral. In those days virality meant that someone at McDonald's heard about it and told a friend who told a friend and so on.

Soon I was playing hostess to a very large soiree. People I thought were friends turned out to be bad, messy drunkards. At the end of the night, which was actually the break of dawn, I was left with the mess to end all messes. It took ten hours to clean up, but not a trace of a party remained. I had vacuumed, repaired, and obliterated the leftover chaos.

When they came home, the coast was clear. They had no idea what had happened only hours before their return. My lips were sealed, and my brother wasn't talking since he had his first taste of booze and girls at twelve years old. I was so thankful, and cocky.

Three days later, I was ignorantly comfortable with my conquest until the village Nosey Parker caught wind of my party. She made a sleazy move to inform my mother, casually but with a stench of arrogance (maybe because her daughter wasn't invited).

My mom answered the phone and all I heard was, "Of course I knew about the party. My daughter and I have a very open relationship. I'm not sure what your concern is."

Oh, snap! Take that Mrs. Parker.

After hanging up the phone, my mother sauntered over to me. She put the town gossip at bay, but she had to deal with me.

I immediately pleaded guilty, but also somehow finessed into her agreeing that it was awfully rude for someone to rat me out like that.

"I mean ... that was awesome, how you told her off like that ... *Mom*?"

"Darling, I know all about your party," she matter-of-facted me.

"What? How?" I was still a child in wonder of adult ways.

"Because, I obviously taught you how to recycle, but not getting rid of the bin was a huge mistake." A Cheshire Cat-like smile settled on her satisfied face.

Son of a &*@$#!

Surprisingly, she wasn't mad.

"Why didn't you say anything? Aren't you angry?" I treaded.

"I'm not impressed, but I figured with the number of bottles a lot of people showed up. Somehow you managed to whip the house back into shape. I don't know how you did it, but I'm assuming it took a very long time. Knowing how much you hate cleaning, I'm guessing that's punishment enough."

I'm nowhere near the confrontation ninja that my mom is, but I have my moments. Even if they are spent wishing I'd said something really good. Naturally, I always have great comebacks hours later.

My mother gave me the statements to make, the timing to deliver, and the wits to use them wisely. This has been more useful than wearing clean underwear every day, because sometimes the laundry doesn't get done. And, in my opinion, panties are technically reversible.

Angila Peters is a freelance writer living in Ingersoll, Ontario. She is a featured writer on *BLUNTmoms*, can be found on *The Huffington Post*, and is a published author in the anthology *Surviving Mental Illness Through Humor*. Her three children are well-nourished considering her blogging habits on *Detached From Logic*, where she pens her own trials and triumphs.

Love is Her Shield

By Autumn Jones

My new bike was a shiny blue and white ten-speed. The thin wheels were fresh with the smell of new rubber. This bike—the gift I had been begging for—was a symbol of my coming of age. It seemed only appropriate that a twelve-year-old girl move from the childish ways of the banana seat to sit upon the tiny sophisticated seat of a bike with shifting gears. I felt powerful as I pedaled swiftly, hearing the chain clunk along as I moved my gear-dial from one to two, and so on, until I reached ten. When top speed was reached, I slowly lifted my hands from the safety of the handlebars, steadying myself on the tiny sophisticated seat, and extended my arms wide to catch the wind. My mother didn't approve when I showed her my trick. She warned me of broken bones and bloody knees. It was one of the duties of parenthood—protecting your child.

I quickly learned that if I wanted to feel the high of riding hands free, I needed to do so a few streets over. Like a junkie who lurks in dark places pursuing a dealer, I pedaled out of sight and on to an adjacent street, where I was free to indulge in my fix. One particularly sunny, Saturday afternoon, I craved the force of wind against my changing body. I was hungry for the freedom that rode tandem, as I took to the road alone. Staying within the boundaries my parents set, I was free to ride as I pleased through the neighborhood. I passed the familiar homes of neighbors, weaved around parked cars, and raced the dogs that chased me down their side of the fence.

As I approached a friend's house, I noticed something out of the ordinary on her sidewalk: chalk drawings. The names of a few neighborhood girls were scrawled in fanciful lettering. I wondered why I had not been invited to the gathering. I pulled over to take a closer look. The sidewalk was a chalky mural of peace signs, stars, and flowers. Hopscotch ran the length of the driveway. As my eyes scanned the images, my brain sent an alert that it had spotted my name. "Autumn is gay and pees on herself," mushroomed up from a pond of happy doodles.

I raced home on my bike, tears heavy with betrayal and dejection soaking my cheeks. Immediately, I told my mother about my discovery. She headed to the garage devoid of hesitation. Grabbing her own bike, she pedaled down the road at lightning speed—me working hard to keep up. We reached the scene of the crime. Everything was exactly as I'd left it five minutes before. It was not a figment of my imagination. Seeing those words a second time stung, but it was not as sharp because my mother was with me. I did not know if she had a plan; I had no preconceived ideas about what she might do. I just knew that having her there absorbed some of the fragments of pain. Her presence made the wound become tolerable.

Her outrage was palpable, as she stormed up to the porch and pounded her fist against the door. "I want you to wash this off. *Right now*," she commanded, pointing to the sidewalk slander. The other mother seemed perplexed, even slightly amused, to see my mother in such an uproar. Minutes later, my "friend" appeared outside with a hose. With my mother's arm around my shoulders, we watched as the words turned to pink and purple streams, flowing into the grass.

On that particularly sunny Saturday afternoon, I had set out to spread my wings, only to have them clipped. I rushed to the solace of my mother, so she could reassemble my broken pieces. She did not tell me what to do, what to say, what to think. Instead, she showed me how to love.

"I want you to wash this off. *Right now*."

Wash this off.

Wash this off.

Right.

Now.

My mother, positioning herself closer to the fire so the flames could not singe me. My mother, announcing her position as the bravest warrior in her daughter's army. What my mother really wanted to wash off was my pain, my embarrassment. She wanted to watch my anguish run off into the grass with the whispers of those cruel words. This is how she loves: bold and unashamed.

"I want you to wash this off. *Right now*."

I stood in awe of my mother. She had done this for me. She had righted the wrong. The thought of her appearing manic or perhaps damaging a relationship with a neighbor was nothing my mother was concerned with. Other peoples' perceptions of her behavior never crossed my mother's mind when it came to protecting me or anyone she loved. As the oldest of four sisters, my mother was long seasoned in the art of loving action before I arrived in her life; a lifetime of rehearsals preparing her for her greatest role: mother.

My personal journey has been an accumulation of my mother laying down her life for me, in various forms and locations. Knowing my mother was my relentless ally was not an epiphany—the idea did not come to me in a rush of knowing. My mother is not a woman of words, but one of action. Her primal compulsion to protect me was (and is) unyielding. The innate duty to keep me safe was born in her when I was birthed from her. It was the moment she gained possession of her primordial shield—the one she passed down to me when I became a parent and found myself in the role of warrior. And as long as I carry her shield, I carry her love.

Autumn Jones is a writer, storyteller, yoga enthusiast, and information hoarder. Although she's a Florida girl at heart, she has fallen in love with the rolling hills of Tennessee. She lives in Nashville with her husband and two boys.

Things My Mother Told Me

By Caroline Sposto

My mother was born in Lake City, Minnesota in 1916.

On the occasion of her ninety-fifth birthday in 2011, I gave her a list of ninety-five things she taught me over the years. She passed away on October 4, 2012. Here are some of the highlights from that list:

1. Never trust anyone or anything that seems too contrived.
2. Don't turn in sloppy homework—and this goes for things that might count as "homework" after you're out of school.
3. If you like birds in your backyard, you can't get a cat. If you get a cat, you can't feed the birds. The whole world works on this kind of rule, if you think about it.
4. If you give the average person hell for mistreating you once, they won't dare do it again.

5. Always count your change, and never automatically pay any fee that you don't understand.
6. There are a lot of stupid people in the world. Get used to it.
7. When you have a big, daunting job ahead of you, separate it into the smallest tasks and get them done one by one. It's scientific, because you'll get a natural boost of adrenaline every time you're about to finish each little task.
8. Women of character are never bored.
9. Go outdoors, you'll feel better.
10. Marriage can be very boring. Understanding this and coping with it is half the battle.
11. We teach our children more by accident than we do by design.
12. There's no fool like an old fool.
13. Once you get to a certain age, most articles in most popular women's magazines, are just more of the same old drivel.
14. If the restaurant doesn't have clean windows, don't eat there.
15. Learn at least enough about how your car runs to allow you to carry on an intelligent conversation with your repairperson. The same goes for every system in your house.
16. Be polite. Always.
17. Don't swear beyond "hell" and "damn" if you can help it.
18. Your handwriting is a reflection of your personality.
19. You don't really know who anybody is until you've been to their house. *Keep this in mind when you keep your house.*

20. Don't ever believe anyone who says: "It doesn't matter how you look."
21. Watch how your speaking voice sounds—it can easily stay the youngest, most attractive part of your body.
22. Even if you don't have much time to stay abreast of the news, at least keep up on the local news.
23. When you write, say what you mean and use simple words.
24. You don't have to marry for money—but if you don't marry a person with the skill, desire, and work ethic to earn a living, you're a silly fool.
25. Don't expect your emotions about anything or anyone to be clear-cut—they hardly ever will be. It's making decisions with mixed emotions that leads to wisdom.
26. Be very careful about the way you talk to people. Everyone is a good deal more fragile than they let on.
27. People don't age in a straight line. When life is hard, we look a little older, and when the hard times pass, we look a little younger again. In other words, don't fix your wrinkles; fix your life and the wrinkles will take care of themselves.
28. Don't smoke. You can mess with a lot of things, but you can't mess with how much oxygen you get.
29. Never be less than you are.
30. *There is such a thing as being too good to people.* When you are, they don't fully appreciate it, and it wears you out.
31. Psychologically, most people have to look the way they have to look, so if you see eccentricities in dress, hair, etc. don't judge—just understand that this is what's going on.
32. Sing every song as if it were your last.

Caroline Sposto began writing in earnest four years ago when her daughters went off to college. Her work has appeared in *The Saturday Evening Post*, *Family Circle*, and publications internationally. She's a Memphis correspondent for Broadwayworld.com and the Poetry Editor for the *Humor in America* blog. In 2011, she was chosen to participate in the Moss Fiction Workshop at the University of Memphis with Richard Bausch. In 2013, she won second place in the Great American Think-Off. She spent the summer of 2014 as a writer in residence at the Helene Wurlitzer Foundation in Taos, New Mexico. She feels grateful; a wistful turning point in life became a happy adventure!

The Beauty in Our Mistakes

By Alison Huff

I remember looking through my family's photo albums as a teenager and coming to the realization that my mother had lived an entirely different life before either of her children were born. It was a startling thing, discovering that she had once been her own person. I saw photos of a rebellious young woman who was as much of a stranger as she was familiar to me, with wide eyes and a captivating smile. She appeared to be a really fun, outgoing, and carefree person who didn't tell people to do the dishes or clean their bedrooms. Instead, she looked like someone I would have wanted to skip school with.

My mother became a licensed beautician during the early 1970s, and a part of her training involved experimenting on real hair. If you've ever had your hair done at a beauty school as an inexpensive alternative to visiting an established salon, you'll probably remember having to sign a potentially dangerous waiver which states that you fully understand the risks involved when you allow inexperienced students to make alterations to your crowning glory.

There are so many things that can go wrong with a haircut, a perm, or a color treatment, and at one time or another, my mother experienced most of them on her own head. She's worn an indeterminate number of hair colors and styles throughout her lifetime, many of which were documented in the old albums I adored looking through. One of my favorite snapshots is a candid photo of my father who, with a dismayed facial expression and latex-gloved hands, can be seen applying some sort of chemical mixture to her accidentally canary-yellow hair.

She never hesitated to try new styles and colors because, as she would later explain, "It's only hair. It will grow back." My mother always knew that mistakes might happen, but with the right solution and a little luck, they could usually be fixed. If not, well—there was always a wig for that.

I inherited my mother's fearlessness. She flaunted rich burgundy tresses long before they were considered haute. I also inherited my mother's follicular restlessness; apparently the burning desire for ever-changing hair was branded deeply within the strands of my DNA. When I was eleven years old, I lusted after Whitney Houston's shoulder-length curls in her music video for "I Wanna Dance with Somebody (Who Loves Me)." My mother did her best to give them to me with my very first perm.

I absolutely loved it. For about a week. The novelty of it soon wore off, the byproduct of my typical pre-teen fickleness.

At some point, I also sported a super-short feathered haircut—one which had a very long rat tail sprouting from the nape. My hair was business in the front and 1980s punk party in the back. I had the longest rat tail in my entire class, and all of the boys marveled at the way I could wrap it around my ear four times. Four times! It was truly epic. At least, that's what I tell myself now. I honestly don't know what I was thinking when I asked for that one; I really wish I did.

Like my mother's, my head could star in its own "Evolution of Hair" YouTube video. It has worn every color and style you can imagine: long merlot waves; beaded micro braids; a loosely curled, deep purple bob; a messy bright blue shag. I can tell you from first-hand experience that the phrase "Once you go black, you'll never go back" is the absolute truth; permanent black dye is impossible to lift without destroying your hair in the process. That was a lesson well-learned.

The first time I attempted to do my own highlights at home, I ended up with a shade that I can only describe as "Tropicana Orange with Fried Lemony Streaks." Several years later, I bravely tried self-highlighting again, because I thought for sure it would turn out differently. It did—this time my hair was far more yellow than it was orange. In one swift, decisive move, I threw caution to the wind and took a set of electric clippers to my grossly over-processed hair. I dyed what was left and I discovered that, every once in a while, an unholy mess that began as a tragic mistake held the potential to turn into something really beautiful in the end.

I rocked that hot pink pixie cut for six months before I finally grew tired of it.

My mother's phrase "It's only hair" took on a much deeper meaning for me as I grew older. Eventually, I realized that there is an absolute impermanence to life; like the sea, it is always in motion, it is always changing, and we cannot predict with any certainty what the next tide will bring. There is a palpable feeling of serenity that comes with resigning to the notion that nothing will last forever. Bad hair. A gnarly pimple. Heartbreak.

Anger. Sadness. Disappointment in myself, disappointment in others. I am able to take great comfort in the knowledge that such obstacles will eventually resolve, if given enough time, making room for better things that will one day fill the voids they left behind.

I owe my optimism and inner peace to those words I took to heart so many years ago, "It's only hair."

Life has an incredibly large learning curve, and it doesn't come with an owner's manual. We are not perfect—not a single one of us—but our errors do not define who we are. There is an immeasurable value to be gathered from the wreckage of our mistakes; with every vital lesson we gain from them, we grow just a little bit more. Our blunders offer a free supply of narratives, little anecdotes of what-not-to-do that we can tuck away in our story-telling arsenals to educate, entertain, and possibly terrify other people whenever the need arises.

I have learned how to embrace my flubs, to seek and apply solutions that might fix the problems that result from them, and, if those don't work, to consider finding a new approach altogether. Whatever happens, I will not allow my past mistakes to steer me away from taking chances at any point in my life because it is impossible to know exactly how things will turn out in the end.

I own a lifetime full of lapses in good judgment and indiscretions, but I have not one single regret to speak of. I will remain as fearless as my mother because after all is said and done, *"It's only hair."*

Mother of Doom and Destruction, **Alison Huff** is an artist and writer who lives a country bumpkin life with her husband, Whovian, in bipolar northeastern Ohio. She is not a morning person. You can read some of her essays on *BLUNTmoms* and also on her blog, *Please Stop Putting Crackers Down My Shirt.*

Support Can Be Beautiful

By Linda Roy

You know that moment when your kid starts yammering on about the video game he's playing, giving you the play-by-play, in minute detail, until your eyes glaze over and surrender into a steady stream of "uh-huhs," all the while thinking, "Sweet baby Jesus, I have no idea what he's talking about?"

My mother never did that.

No, seriously. It didn't matter how trivial, boring, inconsequential, random, rambling, or self-serving it was (and believe me, it was), she would give me full-eye contact and listen. I mean *really* listen, as if she was interested and everything. Of course, sometimes she was. But when your thirteen-year-old daughter is inconsolable because Shaun Cassidy just married a Playboy Bunny, that's heavily encroaching on insipid territory, which I do believe is fair game for a few head nods and "uh-huhs."

My mother is the best listener I know. She laughs at my stupid jokes, endures my complaints, and always lets me know that what's important to me is important to her.

So when I decided at age seven that I wanted to be a singer and musician someday, my mom signed me up for guitar lessons; thus beginning a long and tireless journey: shuttling me to and from lessons of some sort—whether guitar, voice, or flute—and waiting patiently in a music store for me to finish, while the strains of some kid butchering "Stairway to Heaven" hung in the air like some inherent storm cloud.

I became the quirky little performer of the family, always putting on some sort of show or another. "Come listen to my impression of 'Roseanne Roseannadanna,' Mom!" or, "Hey, I wrote a new song. Wanna hear it?" And she'd always come and listen, offering biased or unbiased support and encouragement.

From the time I was very young, I was so into music that I'd pester my mom to take me to concerts. She's attended some real doozies; stuff, that looking back, I don't know how she sat through without the urge to drink heavily. She was there in 1977 when Shaun Cassidy split his skin-tight satin pants while jumping through a paper hoop. She was there for a midnight John Denver show as the opening act, Starland Vocal Band, sang their hit song "Afternoon Delight," a song rife with sexual innuendo, telling me they were just singing about having a midday snack. She even endured a steady downpour so I could see my idol, Linda Ronstadt, in concert, appearing in a scantily clad Boy Scout uniform.

At one point, I decided I wanted to see my guitar teacher's band play at the local VFW hall. My lessons were held at a communal, hippy household turned music studio. I had a school-girl crush on him. I was ten, and he was in his twenties. I don't know if it was because of that Rex Smith movie, where he plays a guitar teacher singing "You Take My Breath Away" to his much younger student, or because I had dreams of someday hitting the "big time" like that myself, but my mom actually took me.

There we were amidst a sea of hippies and clouds of smoke, the only two people in the room not decked out in leather accessorized with feathered roach clips. My mom was all about supporting my "thing," which has always been arty served up with a side of weird.

After only a year and a half of college, I sat her down and explained that I wanted to move to New York to go to acting school. It took some persuading, but she agreed.

Let it be noted that if you're considering parenthood, it's essential to have a sense of humor—especially if your kid exposes you to some potential "What the what?" situations.

My mother and I went apartment hunting in New York, and whether it was the rooming house in Hell's Kitchen run by nuns ("Those are some tough nuns. Those nuns could cut you!") or the sleazebag hocking jewelry in Times Square, she took it all in stride. I'll never forget being followed five city blocks while this guy tried to sell my mom a hot Gucci watch.

"Hey, Lady! Check it out, check *it* out ... gold watch, twenty dolluhs. Check it out."

"No, thank you." My mother brushed him off.

"Hey, pretty lady. I'll give it to you for fifteen."

"No. No, thank you," she politely declined.

"Aw, c'mon. I'll give you a good deal. Check it out," the sleazebag persisted.

Picture, if you will, my mother, stopping on a dime in the middle of Times Square, turning around, and giving this burly, greasy, hairy-chested dude a *what for* in the kind of firm tone only a mother could impart when you haven't picked up your socks after being asked a million times. "I. DON'T. WANT. IT!" I do think the look of fear on the guy's face was the same one I gave her after she caught me smoking one Saturday night in high school. Pure adrenalized terror.

Once when I invited her to an art show I was doing, she not only showed up, but she chatted up a bunch of the artists. I found her sitting on the floor talking to a guy with a Mohawk, dressed all in leather, who went by the name Dick Head. I'm not gonna lie, it kinda freaked me out. But when she came over to me later and said, "Honey, I just had the best talk with your friend Dick Head," I knew she was going to be okay with my world.

And she was. *She is.* After I formed my band, *Jehova Waitresses*, my Catholic mom came to a bunch of our shows. She'd sit at the bar telling everybody it was her daughter up there. They all called her *Mom*, and she'd tell them when they'd had a little too much to drink and to be careful driving home. "Okay Mom," they'd say.

If I've taken anything away from my mother, it's not only gratitude and appreciation for all the tireless hours of support, encouragement, and laughter she's given me throughout my life and artistic journey, but the lesson that it's important as a parent to really listen to my kids and offer them support and encouragement in all of their endeavors—whether they be potentially zany, impossibly ambitious, quirky as hell, or not at all within my own comfort zone.

Because support can be beautiful.

Cheering kids on no matter what is important to them; it means something. And as a parent, I can learn something from them, branch out a little, meet new and interesting people, have weird and wonderful experiences, and let them know it's okay to be themselves and to go for what they really want in life.

That's one of the most valuable things you can teach a kid.

Also, never buy cheap jewelry from strangers in Times Square.

Linda Roy is a humorist, writer, and musician living in New Jersey with her husband and two boys. Her blog, *elleroy was here*, is funny with a soundtrack, a mix of humor and music. She was named a BlogHer Voice of the Year in 2014 for humor, is a regular contributor to *The Huffington Post* and *Humor Outcasts,* and has contributed to *In the Powder Room, Erma Bombeck Writers' Workshop, BlogHer, Mamapedia, BonBon Break, Project Underblog, Midlife Boulevard, Aiming Low, Funny Not Slutty, Sprocket Ink,* and *The Weeklings.* She was Contributing Editor-in-Chief at *Lefty Pop* and is a co-author of the humor anthology *Clash of the Couples,* as well as the upcoming book *Surviving Mental Illness Through Humor.*

How to Be a Lady, and Why My Husband Will Never Leave Me

By *Alessandra Macaluso*

Like many people, while growing up I always felt my mother was too strict and *way* too uptight. How could I not? She was always on my case: *Don't talk like that. Chew with your mouth closed. Act like a lady. You don't chase boys; let the boys chase you.*

Speaking of boys, I remember her single attempt at "the talk" with me and my sister on that fateful day we became scarred for life. We could tell by the tone of her voice when she called us into her room that something was up. We didn't know what it was, but we knew that it was serious. Were my parents getting a divorce? Did something bad happen, God forbid? We sat on the bed while she paced the room. After a few false starts, she finally stopped in her tracks, looked us dead in the eyes, and in her thick, New York accent said, "Okay, here it is. You listen to me. Your thighs are your two best friends. *They always stick together.* All right? *All right?*" While she occasionally broached the hard topics, she did so in the most "proper" way possible.

I had friends who had cool moms. You know the type. Why couldn't she be like them? The ones who let us go do things, like hang out with the boys, not ask us a million questions, and have to know every minor detail of what we did? When I got a little older and started going out at night with friends, she was always waiting up for me. How I hated when she'd wait up for me! I'd pull into the driveway thinking maybe this would be the night that she wouldn't be watching and waiting. Maybe for once she'd have gone to bed. But there she'd be, peering out the window, a vigilant night owl, with a head full of rollers. Ugh. *Didn't she have better things to do?*

By the time I started driving, they may as well have made a navigation setting in her voice, because that's all I'd hear. "Putcha seat belt on! Watch out for the deer. Stop at this gas station, you're running on FUMES, for cryin' out loud!" And if anyone even so much *thought* about running a stop sign, "You stay RIGHT. THERE. Don't you move!"

When it comes to drinking, I've never actually seen my mother so much as take a sip of an alcoholic beverage. When I was old enough to do so and we'd attend a large family party such as a wedding, my sister and I were all too happy to order glasses of Pinot Grigio and parade them around the event. *Look at us! We're drinking, and we're allowed!* We'd make our way to the dance floor, wine glasses in hand, and bust-a-move with our cousins. What would my mother do? Before we could even get two beats in, she'd hop up from her chair, saunter out onto the dance floor, and pluck the wine glasses from our hands. She'd whisper in our ears, "Don't *ever* bring your drink

out onto the dance floor. You look like a bunch of hussies."
What a buzz kill! We were just having fun!

It seemed that no matter what, she'd always be watching, lips pursed like a live-in "Miss Manners," just waiting to correct our every move. For the most part, I tuned her out—*or so I thought.* Turns out her voice was always playing in the background of my mind, like a late-night infomercial working its way into my psyche when I least expected it. ("I simply *must* have that vegetable chopper for only three small payments of ten dollars and ninety-nine cents! But first, let me put down my wine glass.")

Yet every once in a while, amidst the white noise about being a lady, seatbelts, and not chasing boys, she'd unleash a hidden gem. An unexpected golden nugget of wisdom I could *really* use in life, something that would stick with me forever.

I remember in particular a night when my mother and father bickered at the dinner table. Let me preface this by saying that together they are a comedic act: her with the New York accent and him a born and bred Italian boy who, although he came to America when he was sixteen, somehow still sounds as if he just stepped off the boat. He is a musician, always out playing his saxophone at parties and night clubs, and this particular night he was upset that my mother no longer went to watch him play.

In his thick Italian accent he said, "Why you no come to my gigs anymore?" Then, turning to us, "Your mother, she always used to come watch me. Now? No more. Hasn't come in years. She no want to go out with me anymore either."

My mother pooh-poohed him with a wave of her arm and kept eating.

"No, really. Why not? It would let everyone know I'm taken, you know? You should see the way these women throw themselves at me!"

"Oh, please," she said.

"They do!" Then, after some thought, he began to tease her. "That's it. You know what I'm-a gonna do? I'm-a gonna find me a young girlfriend. Yes, a nice hot young blonde with big fake boobs, and she'll come watch me play the saxophone."

"You go ahead and try it, Joe," she said, glaring from her chair.

"I will! The ladies love me, Jo Ann."

My mother started to say something, but then stopped.

"What?" we all said, encouraging her.

"Nothing. It would just never happen." She crossed her arms and sat there, prim and proper, a demure look on her face.

"What were you going to say?" we pressed. "TELL US!"

"Yes, Jo Ann, why you no think I can get a hot young blondie?"

With my dad egging her on, and the pressure from us, she couldn't take it anymore; she had hit her breaking point. And nobody was prepared for what came bursting out of her mouth.

"You'll never get a younger girlfriend, because NOBODY LIKES AN OLD DICK, Joe!"

My sister, brother, and I fell over laughing. It was simultaneously the grossest and most glorious thing I'd ever heard her say. My father sat there dumbfounded and defeated and to this day has never again brought up the idea of a "hot young blondie."

It was in that moment that I learned that you can indeed follow the rulebook on how to act like a lady, but when applicable, you use it to whack someone upside their head. You then lift your fork, take a dainty bite, and chew with your mouth closed, because you, my dear, are a lady, *and you will be treated like one, dammit.*

The older I get the more thankful I am that my mother was and still is this way. I'm no Miss Manners and, apparently, neither is she. But I've definitely thought twice, and made different decisions, based on the fact that I'd often hear her voice echoing in my mind.

A few years after college, I was out at a bar and saw several girls parading around on a dance floor with their drinks in their hands, the contents spilling out of their glasses, as they swayed back and forth. And I'll be damned, they looked like a bunch of hussies. My mother was right.

When it comes to raising my own little girl, while I will certainly share a drink with her when she is of age, should I ever see her cross a dance floor with one in her hand, you better believe I will confiscate it. As for my husband, should he ever threaten to leave me for a younger woman, I will politely remind him that indeed, "Nobody likes an old dick."

Alessandra Macaluso is author of *The Bitch's Bridal Bible: The Must-Have, Real-Deal Guide for Brides.* Alessandra also writes screenplays and articles and is a blogger for *The Huffington Post.* She has contributed to *Scary Mommy, Uptown Magazine, Charlotte Magazine,* and many other publications, and was featured in *The New York Times* "Life and Style" section. Her original screenplay, *Polar Suburbia,* placed as a semi-finalist in the 2009 Moondance Film Festival. Alessandra is currently working on a cookbook for babies and toddlers called *What a Good Eater!* She's also at work on a book about pregnancy called *Bump Therapy.* For more visit her blog, *Punk Wife.*

Going Solo

By Susie Petersiel Berg

The first time I took a trip by myself—not a business trip, or a weekend with friends, or a writing workshop, but a trip for no reason but to get away—most people were curious. I went to London, England, to visit a friend who was there for two years with her family.

That week was everything I had hoped it would be. During my stay, I spent time on my own for several days, and I also spent a few days with my friend and her family. Talking about my trip later with a long-time friend, I was struck when she said, "You can go back, you know. You can make this something you do for yourself every year." My first thought was, *Holy crap, she's right, I can!* My second thought was, *But what will my parents think?*

Understand, I took this trip when I was forty-four years old. I was married, I had two children, both by then in double digits, and I'd had a solid career as a freelance editor and writer for more than a dozen years. *What would my parents think? Really?*

My parents, as of this writing, have been married for fifty-one years. For at least the first forty-five of those, my father's on-call schedule as an obstetrician/gynecologist notwithstanding, they had never spent a night apart.

None of us knows our parents as young people. By the time we are old enough to recognize that they are not need-filling machines for us, we see them not as people, but as obstacles to having fun, to eating whatever we want, and to beating the stuffing out of our siblings. Then they become entities from whom we are trying to differentiate ourselves. It takes a lot of years, if it ever happens at all, for us to be able to see them objectively.

We can't know what they felt as young marrieds or young parents. What wishes they might have had for their lives, what dreams they thought they might follow, but never did. What compromises they made, happily or unhappily, for us or for one another. By the fixed reality of time, most parents grow up in a generation different from their children. In my parents' case, women had different, and often fewer, options.

My mother was a teacher and lived at a time when she had to quit her job when she had me. She didn't return to the classroom until her youngest child, my brother, was in school all day. During those in-between years, she ran two businesses that appealed to her creative side (cake-decorating classes and an interior decorating business). She put a lot of energy into our home and family. Did she want to disappear for a week on her own to a place where her schedule wasn't dictated by what time dinner had to be in the oven? My guess is you're damn right she did. But the option probably wasn't available to her. Imagine what her parents might have thought.

My father worked a lot of long hours. Doctors don't have nine-to-five shifts; they work overnights and weekends, and they don't run out of the office when a patient is in distress. I know the long hours were worth it to my father, because the joys of his type of medicine generally outweighed the sorrows. But working like that, for both partners, meant that you wanted to spend your downtime with your family and wanted some alone time with your partner. So it was not a surprise to me that my parents never spent time apart.

My parents have had to adjust to being together day and night like most retirees. Over time, they've found the activities and interests that bring meaning to their days. At night, though, they want to return to the place that grounds them. Wherever they are, they are that place for one another.

My life hasn't played out in the same way. My husband and I have both been running our own businesses for close to twenty years now. He works from his parents' home and from his car. For the bulk of our children's lives, there has been someone at home and someone available at any time of the day for medical appointments, forgotten lunch boxes, sick days, and driving to school-team sports events in the least convenient places at the least convenient times. Both of us have always been home by 6:00 p.m., if not earlier. After twenty years of all this presence, I crave absence—absence of responsibility, absence of schedules, and most of all, absence of noise. I cannot access any of these things when I'm in the midst of my family's life and home. I cannot focus on my writing when I need to buy groceries, sign a trip form, or pay the cable bill—usually all three unraveling at the same time.

I did go back to London the following year, though my friend had moved away. I stayed in an apartment hotel and filled my kitchen with tea, ready-made meals from Waitrose, and cherry-walnut bread from the nearby bakery. I searched the city for scones. I went to the Victoria and Albert whenever I felt like it. I walked through areas of London I'd missed the year before. I wrote for at least eight hours a day. I barely spoke a word to anyone. I slept in and then later brought my tea and breakfast into bed while I wrote. I ventured outdoors most days around 1:30 p.m. It was bliss. I did it again the next year, this time in Washington, D.C., at the home of a friend. That week I almost never left the house except for groceries, a nighttime visit to the monuments, and some yoga classes.

One of those classes was scheduled on my final night in Washington. I expected a one-hour vinyasa flow practice, but when I entered the room, I knew from the heat that this was *hot* yoga, which I had never tried. The instructor welcomed us. She began, "For the next seventy-five minutes ..." Hot yoga. Seventy-five minutes. No towel. One of my goals for the week was "no expectations." Okay, I thought. No expectations. If I hated the class, I could leave.

It is no exaggeration to say that those seventy-five minutes were among the most transcendent of my life. The sweat poured off me and pooled into places I didn't know existed. As the class neared its end, the instructor said, "Leave behind everything that doesn't serve you." I was certainly leaving behind a fair volume of sweat. But I was also leaving behind all the expectations that others had of me; all the fears that held me back and kept me from doing what was right for me; all the perceived hurts and slights I'd let harm my soul.

Once or twice a year now, I separate from everyone and everything, so I can focus on my writing and myself. My husband supports me completely. Perhaps my parents find it unnerving, but I have learned what I need to from them. My life is influenced by their connection with each other, by the way I grew up, but I don't need to live in the same place. I know what I need: silence, time, my best and most troubling thoughts, and the grace not to worry what anyone else thinks.

Susie Petersiel Berg is the co-curator of Toronto's Plasticine Poetry Reading Series and the author of the poetry collection *How to Get Over Yourself*, the chapbook *Paper Cuts*, and the blog *The Starbucks Poetry Project*. Her poetry has appeared in such journals as *carte blanche*, *ArsMedica*, and *Switchback*, and in the anthologies *The Mom Egg Review*, *Desperately Seeking Susans*, and *Body and Soul*. Her essay "Through These Eyes" appeared on *Dear Wendy*. Forthcoming are two chapbooks: *You Will Still Have Birds*, a conversation in poetry with Elana Wolff, from Lyrical Myrical Press, and *Awaiting Butterflies* from words(on)pages press. She is a frequent reader on Toronto stages and has also appeared on stage in New York and Philadelphia. Visit her online at: sber40.wix.com/susieberg.

My Superhero Wears a Fuzzy Red Housecoat

By Miranda Gargasz

I sat in my truck waiting in the car-rider line for Tony to come out of school. It was an especially nervous day. A girl named Alyssa, from his grade and about twice his size, had been bullying him relentlessly. He came to the truck most days in tears, because she wouldn't leave him alone. I felt helpless. He felt helpless. I had no idea what I needed to do. The day ended with me channeling my mother in a most epic and terrible way.

The first time Alyssa threatened him was while they were waiting in the car-rider line, inside the building. Tony ignored her at first, hoping she'd stop, but she wasn't deterred. A teacher overheard her cruel words and made her apologize to him. The second time she threatened him was in the lunchroom.

"You're so gay," Alyssa taunted.

"Leave me alone," Tony said.

"That's what gay people say. You like boys."

67

We don't raise our kids to feel that gay people are bad or different, and we have explained to Tony that there are some people who don't necessarily share our viewpoint. Knowing that Alyssa was probably part of that group, he said, "And if I do, would it make you uncomfortable? Should I kiss a boy and see if it makes you puke?"

I immediately got a call from the principal.

"Mrs. Gargasz, there was a small incident today involving Anthony. He was having words with a girl at lunch. We had a talk."

"A talk? What about?"

The principal proceeded to tell me about the conversation and how it led to Alyssa threatening to punch Tony.

"And?" I questioned.

"Well, we talked about not calling people names and not hitting them. Where we have a problem is that Tony doesn't see what he did as wrong."

"I'm sorry? What did he do wrong?"

"Well, he egged her on."

I was silent for a moment before replying. "He was trying to stand up for himself."

"And we talked about that. That's how he saw it. But in that instance he actually became the bully."

By this point, I was pissed, and all constructive conversation went out the window. How does standing up for oneself equate to becoming a bully? What was the alternative choice? Was he just supposed to ignore her? Ignoring her didn't seem to bother her the first time she had a run-in with him. Why would it work now? I resolved to give the girl one more chance. Maybe being called into the principal's office would scare her enough to keep her out of my kid's hair.

No such luck.

The third time she bullied Tony was while they walked to the car-rider line. Her mom parked about four cars ahead of me every day. It was just past the crosswalk that Alyssa waited to get in Tony's face. Blocked from my view by other cars, I couldn't see what she did. By the time Tony made it to the truck he was sobbing and mucus was running from his nose.

"I don't want to go to school anymore. I can't take this, Mom. She pushed me down on the ground. Now she's saying that she is going to get a bunch of her friends to beat me up."

I drove to the school immediately. The principal wasn't available to meet with me, so I was sent home to stew in my juices all evening. I did my best to reassure Tony that I would fix this. She would stop doing this, come hell or high water.

At night as I lay in bed, I wracked my brain about what to do. All I could think of was my mother's reaction to bullies when I was a kid.

In first grade, when I was about six years old, I had to walk to a bus stop to get picked up for school. I didn't grow up in the best neighborhood, and there were kids of all ages who waited there with me. One girl, around three years ahead of me in school, decided that I was shy enough to be the butt of her every joke. Her older sister waited with us and ignored everything she did. They had an older brother who was usually there, but he'd recently been sent away for various crimes. She threatened me and pushed me in the dirt every single day. She frightened me to death.

I remember coming home in tears, telling my mom about her.

"You've got to stand your ground. Don't let her bully you," my mom said.

Each day I'd walk to the bus stop, and each day she'd do the same thing. My mom tried talking to her parents, but each time she knocked on their door, she was ignored.

Tired of the shenanigans, my mom approached me one morning before school. She had a thin, oblong rock in her hand. She took my book bag and slid the rock inside. "She starts her shit this morning, you cold-cock the little bitch." I felt my eyes bulge out of my head. "I'll be watching," she said, as she pulled the tie of her fuzzy red housecoat tighter.

I trudged to the bus stop, the rock weighing down my Kermit the Frog book bag. I felt powerful and wrong all at the same time. I stopped at our spot, and seconds later the girl came after me. I stood my ground. Just as she was about to push me, I swung back with my book bag, doing as my mother bid me. Not only did she have to deal with the bells I'm sure she heard blasting in her ears, but like a caped crusader, my mom was suddenly standing next to me. Her housecoat was wide open to reveal her street clothes and no longer the nightgown.

"Go home, little girl," my mother bawled. "There's more where that came from. Just cuz she's little don't mean she can't whoop your ass."

Go home she did, crying and screaming. Her sister was in too much shock to follow her.

My mom grabbed my chin and winked at me.

"I got dressed before you this morning. I put my housecoat on so she wouldn't think I'd do anything if she saw me at the window." With that, she walked away.

Every kid at the bus stop stood in silence, looking at me with bug eyes. No one ever bothered me again.

It was that memory that got me to sleep that night thinking about Tony.

The thought of a physical altercation turned my stomach. Determined to exhaust all my possibilities first, I called the principal the next morning.

"Mrs. Gargasz, I'm sorry, but I can't be responsible for behavior that happens off the school grounds."

"You mean to tell me that this girl can beat my son up two steps from the damn crosswalk, and you won't do a thing about it?"

"I have no rights once they're off school property. I also have no way of knowing if Tony instigated anything or if she did in fact react the way he says she did."

My jaw was clenched so tightly I thought I was going to break a tooth. I hung up, knowing that I was never going to get anywhere with the principal.

I sat there that day, in the car-rider line, waiting and watching.

Alyssa came out of the building before Tony. She waited by her car, which Tony would have to walk by to get to me. Her mother wasn't in their car, because Alyssa's baby sister was a kindergartener and had to be walked out of the building by a parent.

Tony came out a few minutes later, and damned if Alyssa didn't trot up to him, running her mouth, with her face only an inch away from his. She continued to follow Tony until she was about a foot from the front of my truck. She gave him a little shove between his shoulder blades, before she walked off saying, "I'm gonna beat you up tomorrow. Me and my friends at recess. Wait and see." Then she turned and popped him the middle finger.

Mama Bear rose in me like she never had before. My mother's fuzzy red housecoat flashed before my eyes. I saw Alyssa's mom return and get back into her car.

"Tony, get in the truck and buckle up. Now."

Sniffling, he did as he was bid.

I slammed the truck into gear, pounded the gas, and squealed off, blocking their car in with my vehicle. Her mother stared at me wide-eyed.

"Alyssa is your daughter?" I asked, through pinched lips, my nostrils flaring.

"Yes," the woman said.

"Every day she comes out of school and threatens my son. She swears at him like a sailor and puts her hands on him. This is the fourth time this has happened, and the school refuses to do anything about it. Lady, I'm here to tell you that I'm not that patient."

"The principal led me to believe that he is instigating it."

"The principal is wrong. She literally waited for him to come out of school today and threatened him right in front of me."

"Well, what happens off school property happens. I'm sure she was just teasing."

In that instant Mama Bear sprouted horns.

"Let me break this down for you. She so much as breathes wrong in his general direction, and I'm going to let him hand her her ass. I don't care if she's a girl. He's been in karate for two years now. He's not allowed to use it to fight, but I'll give him permission. Do you want to see your daughter in a straight-arm bar? It's not pretty, and it happens to be a move he's really good at. It won't hurt her, but it will sure embarrass the shit out of her. No matter how much she screams or cries she won't get out of it. He'll keep her there until the cops come. So it's up to you and Alyssa." With that, I peeled off.

I went home and hated myself for my behavior. I didn't want to threaten and bully, but that's exactly what I'd done. I did have a few thoughts to console me. First, those who were charged with the task were not protecting my son. Instead of creating a safe haven for him, his pleas for help, and mine, were continually ignored. It was my opinion that in his own way the principal was a bit of a bully too. By failing to *really* listen and address the problem, he left my son helpless while empowering Alyssa to continue her behavior. Second, I had exhausted every other possibility to rectify the situation.

Ultimately, though, the responsibility for showing my son that adults are supposed to protect him, to allow him to stand up for himself, and to give him an example of the right way to follow through conflict-resolution fell to me. While I don't condone violence, it still has to be said that life is sticky, and sometimes the resolution can be distasteful but overwhelmingly effective.

I realized it was not my finest parenting moment. But it worked. Alyssa never bothered him again. I may just need to purchase my own fuzzy red housecoat.

Miranda Gargasz is a writer from a small suburb outside Cleveland, Ohio. She previously earned a degree in Elementary Education. Her essays have appeared in *The Christian Science Monitor* and on HumorPress.com. In 2014, she published her first collection of essays called *Lemonade and Holy Stuff.* Since publishing her book, she has become a contributor to *The Huffington Post, ModernMom,* and the popular mom site *What The Flicka?,* the brain-child of actress Felicity Huffman. She's also been featured on *Mamapedia.* She lives with her husband, two sons, and a feisty mutt. You can visit her at Mirandagargasz.wordpress.com.

Mother Knows Best (Really!)

By Teri Biebel

We're all guilty. If you don't agree, you're either lying to yourself or you're full of crap. Our mothers really DO know what they're talking about. Sometimes it just takes us a little longer to realize this. For me, it took about twenty years.

My parents divorced when I was seven. My mom, my brother, and I lived at the Jersey Shore (not the Snooki/J-Wow Jersey Shore, so get that image out of your head). Wildwood was our hometown, and it was a very quiet and fun place to grow up. Summers in our little burg were crazy; winters were peaceful. My mom had started seeing someone after her divorce, and he seemed like a nice enough guy. He was a roofer by trade and a reformed alcoholic. Their relationship was a good, solid one for several years, until they got married. I was in eighth grade.

Things changed rapidly after the wedding. His long-lost brother came back into his life; that's when the drinking started up again. My stepfather hadn't had a drink in more than twenty years, but when he reconnected with his brother, the drinking began again, in earnest. He seemed to be making up for lost time. He'd go out on a roofing job at 7:00 a.m., and sometimes he wouldn't stumble in at home until after 11:00 at night, drunk off his ass. We could always tell what he'd been drinking by his mood. Drinking beer meant he was in a friendly mood. If he came home yelling and angry, it meant hard liquor. He was a mean, nasty drunk when liquor was involved, and it was never pretty.

I can remember being up in my room listening to him berate my mother using awful language. I can remember the first time my mother shot back at him and the knot in my stomach when she used the F-word. My mother detested that word, so when she used it, I knew she meant business. She allowed him to continue his behavior, and I couldn't understand why.

It became a pattern. She'd throw him out. He'd say he would straighten up. She'd take him back. Rinse. Repeat. Ad nauseam. This went on for years. Originally, after the wedding he was going to adopt me, and I was going to take his last name. The wedding was in April, and the legal adoption process started in May. By the time I started high school in September, I wanted nothing to do with him, or his last name, and went through the whole process of UNDOING what we had started. I kept my name and hated him. I hated him all through high school. To this day, I still have no good thoughts about or toward him.

I remember when I was sixteen, and Mom was taking him back for the forty-hundredth time. I confronted her, crying, asking her why? Why would she continue to put herself through the anguish? It was an ugly cartoon on a never-ending loop. Her response to me was, "When you're older and you fall in love, you'll understand."

And at that time, I thought she was full of crap. I always said to myself there was NO WAY I'd put up with a husband like that. NO WAY would I allow someone I was in love with to get away with the things he'd done.

Just before I graduated from high school, she left him for good. We sold our house and moved to the Atlantic City area. I went off to college and between my freshman and sophomore years, I got a part-time summer job at one of the big casinos. I made some new friends and more money than I had ever made working as a waitress on the Wildwood Boardwalk. I also met my first real boyfriend, or as I call him, my FRB.

FRB was gorgeous. He was sweet, well-liked—and *gorgeous*. After we began dating, I would come home from college on the weekends, stay at his apartment, and work part-time at the casino. It was then that I found out that FRB had a little side business going. Unsafe and illegal. I turned a blind eye to this little business and went about working and going to school. If I didn't see it, it didn't happen, right?

I left college in the middle of my sophomore year, and FRB and I got an apartment together. I made it clear before we moved in that I would NOT allow anything illegal in my house. So if he had anything, he had to get rid of it. I was not into the stuff he was selling, and I would NOT be arrested as an accessory to a crime, so I put my foot down. He obliged, and we lived happily ever after—for a year. Then I found something in his pocket. The same something I distinctly forbid him to bring into our home. I went home from work that night and tore our apartment apart. I checked suitcases, took clothes out of drawers, and looked in shoeboxes. I even checked inside of socks. I was beyond livid.

Not long after that FRB and I broke up. He moved back home to live with his parents, and I moved on with my life. Fast forward twenty years to lunch with my fifteen-year-old daughter. We were discussing how some women put up with certain behavior from their boyfriends and why some women allow certain behavior while others don't. I explained to her that my mom always said, "When you're older and in love, you'll understand." And THAT'S when it hit me. It hit me like a freight train. I had stuck with FRB and his illegal activities because I loved him. Sure, I had ended the relationship when I caught him breaking his promise. But prior to our living together, I had overlooked it because I loved him. Holy crap, Mom was right, and I didn't realize it until twenty years later!

I am so thankful that my mom is still here so that I can tell her how right she was, even if it took a conversation with my own daughter to realize it. Better late than never, *right*? And hopefully my own daughters won't take nearly that long to realize that I, too, know what I'm talking about.

Teri Biebel is a working mom, with two teenage daughters. She is a *New York Times* bestselling author, a writer, a ranter, a fan-girl, and has a huge crush on Mike Rowe. You can find her at the blog, *Snarkfest*.

Criticize Your Child to Better Self-Esteem

By Gillie Bishop

My mom is yelling at me, our argument whipping her into an angry frenzy. The conflict is an ancient one between us. I believe that I should set goals and improve myself. She believes that I should be happy with the way things are.

"This is your problem," she says, grinding her teeth. "When you measure your success against outcomes, you're more likely to be disappointed. You can only control what *you* do, not the outcomes."

"I guess," I say. "But is it sort of pointless to keep doing something if you're not getting the outcomes you want?"

"No!" she cries, furious now. "You have to enjoy the process! You can only do what you think is right and not worry about the outcomes!"

I try to remain calm and cool. "I see what you're saying, but when you're trying to accomplish something, don't you need to pay attention to whether it's working?"

"I'm trying to teach you how to feel good about yourself," she shouts. "I just want you to have good self-esteem!"

I was a cautious, self-improvement-obsessed child who grew into a (surprise!) cautious, self-improvement-obsessed adult. I've always had schedules for selecting my outfits and managing my time and living up to my New Year's resolutions. My mom scoffs at these systems. "Anything worth doing," she assures me, "is worth doing half-assed."

And yet, sometimes doing things half-assed upsets her too. Once, she freaked out when I overcooked the sauce for the pasta carbonara we were making for dinner guests. When she saw the tiny bits of cooked egg floating in the sauce, she panicked about the ruined meal. Although I was over thirty years old at the time, and the mother of a toddler, I became an indignant child. It was my in-laws coming to dinner, not the Queen. The tiny chunks of egg in the sauce wouldn't affect the taste. I didn't see what the big deal was.

The next day, my mom apologized for being so critical. "It's hard for me to see you make mistakes in cooking," she said. "Cooking is something I'm good at, and I feel responsible for your ignorance about it."

As a daughter, I resented the implication that I was an "ignorant" cook just because I overcooked an egg. But as a mother, I knew that feeling. How many times already, in my year and a half as a parent, had I agonized about what my daughter's bad behavior might say about me? Was she having a tantrum because I hadn't brought a snack to the library? Was she tearing all the books off the bookshelf because I hadn't modeled care for belongings? Was she hesitant to respond to friendly adults because she'd observed my own social awkwardness?

As my daughters (now twelve and nine) have gotten older, I've found more and more ways in which their faults reveal my inadequacy. A glance in the back seat of my car proves I've raised privileged brats who don't value their belongings. Their messy hair advertises how little I know or care about beauty, as well as my selfishness. (Clearly, I spend the half hour before school eating breakfast instead of brushing anyone's hair.) Their failure to call their friends is eerily reminiscent of my own shyness.

If Maggie and Brynn are bad at something I'm bad at, I'm a poor role model. If they're bad at something I'm good at, there's no excuse for how badly I've let them down. So I nag, yell, and worry, trying to fix them so they'll make me feel like a good mother and trying to fix them so they won't be unhappy.

My mother was an above-average student with two siblings who were academic standouts. When I was in high school, she often reminded me that I didn't have to maintain my nearly straight-A average. "It wouldn't kill you to get a B once in a while," she said. Her intention, I see now, was to relieve me of the academic pressure she'd felt. But to me, the message was: *Why are you such a geek? Why can't you be cooler and excel at something besides school?* It was all part of her plot to turn me into the cool daughter she wished she'd had.

I've parlayed my nerdy and uncool vision of myself into my own projection now that Maggie has started middle school. I've worked hard to assure Maggie that she's awesome just the way she is and doesn't need to get swept up in the image-consciousness of youth. Before she started seventh grade, I asked my Facebook friends to share advice they wished they'd gotten at Maggie's age. As I read her the warnings about mean girls, and the "It's okay to be nerdy" advice, I could see that her primary reaction was pity for me and my insecure friends. My geeky-cool rock-n-roll drummer girl was not anticipating similar challenges to her self-esteem.

But how can we *not* try to save our children from pain, either real or imagined? Seeing that I felt insecure about my appearance, my mom tried to encourage me to wear a little makeup in high school—which, of course, led me to feel that she thought I was ugly and unsatisfied with the way I was. Her yelling at me to have better self-esteem comes from the same place as her desire to help me feel better about my appearance. She wants me to be free from disappointment, and the best way to protect myself from it is to avoid expectations. She has been trying to protect me in this way my whole life and never seems to catch a break. Instead, she hurts my feelings, makes me mad, and becomes the villain in bad mother horror stories. The most famous is the time that I told her I wanted to be a songwriter. I was sixteen at the time. "But, Gill, you have no musical ability! Why don't you be a poet instead?" she said.

She was right, of course. I really didn't have much musical ability. But did she say this because I really didn't have a natural gift for music or (as a little piece of me has always suspected) because no one ever encouraged me in this area? (Let's forget, for the moment, the years of piano lessons and children's choir.) Was there still hope at sixteen? If my mom had run out and signed me up for a songwriting class, might I have found untapped musical talent? Might I be in Nashville or New York writing songs, instead of in Denver writing this essay?

My nine-year-old daughter, Brynn, has told me that she wants to be an elephant keeper when she grows up. She has a room full of elephant stuff. She's read every book in her school library about elephants. She can tell you the names, continents of origin, and ages of all the elephants at the Denver Zoo. She sponsors two elephants at an African sanctuary for orphaned elephants. She's smart and able-bodied. But, if you ask me, she'll never be an elephant keeper.

She loves elephants because she loves relationships. She loves the idea of nurturing something cute and sensitive. She loves nurturing, in general. I see this every time she hugs me or tells me how much she loves me. I see this in the way she tucks her favorite necklaces into bed at night and assigns names and personalities to her water bottles. I see this in the way she asks me questions about how I felt at the hardest points in my life: *Were you sad when Gramps and Frammar got divorced? What was it like when your best friend died of colon cancer? How old were you when your grandparents died? Did you cry?*

My twelve-year-old daughter, Maggie, would never ask these uncomfortable questions. It doesn't occur to her to wonder, and she prefers to keep emotions on an even keel. But Maggie is observant and thoughtful, always noticing and integrating information. When Maggie was around five years old, she told me, "Mom, I can tell just by the smell of my poop what color it's gonna be!" I knew then that she would be—that she already *was*—a naturalist. She has pondered the chicken-and-egg question through the lens of evolution. She's taught me the finer points of our dogs' body language. She's explained to me how dogs domesticated themselves in the distant past. *This* is the child who may become a zookeeper one day. Brynn should be a therapist or an actress—or maybe a poet.

I see where my mom was coming from. Why should I waste time trying to write a song and probably failing? Instead, I could be crafting poems and possibly succeeding. Anyone who's heard me sing or play piano can see that I'm more likely to have success with words. Why should Brynn waste time pretending she's interested in feeding and cleaning up after elephants? Anyone can see that she will have more fun connecting with other people and exploring emotions.

And yet, it hurt when my mom told me I shouldn't write songs. It didn't feel like she was cluing me in to my deeper passions. Her admonition to give up on outcomes never feels like sound psychological advice, but rather a huge vote of no-confidence. And so it must be when I offer sage, unsolicited advice to my kids about how *they* could be better and happier—when I nag them about their messiness or worry over their friendships.

What is the antidote to this problem in the mother-daughter relationship? Appropriately enough, my answers have come from my own mother. She told the story of yelling at me to have better self-esteem in a sermon she wrote—a sermon titled "Deep Listening." She suggested that, instead of trying to make me see the wisdom in letting go of outcomes, she could have listened more, to learn about where my feelings were coming from. If I had felt heard and gently challenged to explore my motivations, maybe I would have been able to let go of the outcomes on my own. Certainly, I would have felt more loved and supported by my mom.

And I wonder what might've happened if, instead of warning me that I had no musical ability, she had said, "You want to be a songwriter? Why?" Maybe I would have come around to the truth—that I loved words and inspiration and *should* be a poet, instead of stewing about how little my mom thought of my abilities.

What if she had congratulated me on my straight-A report card and then gently asked, "How do *you* feel about getting straight A's? Does it feel like there's a lot of pressure on you to do well?" Might I have been able to take her concern at face value, instead of feeling like she was wishing for a different kind of child?

And what about my own children? Can I reflect back what I hear from them without inserting my own advice and opinions? Can I explore with Brynn all the things she would enjoy about elephant keeping without letting on that I don't think she's cut out for it? Can I ask Maggie about her middle school experiences without projecting my own adolescent baggage onto her? And how can I tell if what I'm saying to my children is nurturing or potentially hurtful?

My mom offered me some wisdom here, as well, albeit in a conversation full of bits of conflicting advice. She had been telling me that I really needed to do more to *ensure* that Maggie and Brynn's chores were getting done. When I began to tell her how I was enforcing chores, she did an about-face and said that maybe it was better to not make a big deal or a power struggle out of it. I was just beginning to work myself into a pout (*No matter what I do, you think it's wrong!*), when she hit me with a bit of wisdom. She sighed and said, "If I had to do it all over again, I would spend less time trying to change my child and more time taking care of myself." When I asked what she meant, she said, "I wish I had just set the limits I needed for my own well-being and let you figure out the rest."

And there it is—the egg chunk in the pasta carbonara. We think that it's our jobs as mothers to teach our children to cook, to make friends, to clean up after themselves, to beautify themselves, to be happy, to find careers that suit them, to be successful. But what if, instead, we were able to show them how to fail with grace, to love themselves unconditionally, and to listen without judgment toward themselves and others?

Unfortunately, yelling at them to do these things doesn't work, as my mom discovered. (Haven't we all?) We have to model them, embody them, embrace them. We have to allow ourselves to feel good enough, even when we may be ruining our children right and left. We have to accept that our children will experience pain, disappointment, failure, and low self-esteem. They might embarrass us, or themselves, or make us worry for their mental or physical health. And we must love them and (much harder) ourselves anyway. If we want our kids to have good self-esteem, we might need to quit working so hard toward that objective and allow them to be themselves, low self-esteem and all.

But whatever you do, don't tell my mother she was right!

Gillie Bishop lives, writes, and lovingly criticizes her two tween daughters in Westminster, Colorado. Both kids appear to have pretty good self-esteem, because of or in spite of her. Her writing has appeared in the *UU World* magazine and at uuworld.org.

How Not to Be Overwhelmed by Either Toothpaste or Triplets

By Andrew S. Delfino

Recently I was at a big box store running errands with my toddler. It was a store we don't normally go to, which meant I was a little frazzled keeping the toddler from jumping out of the cart while finding the diapers, soap, and various other items on my list in an unfamiliar place. Eventually we got to the last item: toothpaste. When I did finally locate the aisle, I just stood there for a second, overwhelmed by the insane number of toothpaste options. Something that seems like it should be a simple choice instead has an entire aisle devoted to infinite choices of flavor, texture, and whitening level. Looking for my specific brand is always like an Easter egg hunt, but without any candy or loose change as a reward for finding the right one. On this day, in unfamiliar surrounds, my frustration level rose with each passing second, until I remembered my mother's advice: "No use stressing or complaining about what you've got to do. Just do it and move on with your life." So I picked the nearest toothpaste, closest to the one we usually buy, and moved on.

Following my mother's advice to simply *do what you've got to do and move on* isn't so easy for people these days. Most conversations my wife and I have with our friends include complaints about all the different stressors they have—how overwhelmed they are by chores, errands, or work projects in their lives. For example, one friend is totally overwhelmed by life. Going to a grocery store or having to spend a Saturday waiting for a plumber causes her stress. For every one of her kids' school days off, she builds elaborately detailed spreadsheets of activities for her daughters, so that she can have "all the information" she needs to make the "best decision." She sends out crowd-sourcing emails at 4:30 a.m., stressing about whether we know of any activity, camp, or workshop option that has escaped entry into her spreadsheet. Then she actually has to decide what the girls are going to do, a decision that stresses her out because she has dozens of options. Even something that should be pleasurable, like taking a walk, is not relaxing to her. I once saw her walking down the street on a beautiful Sunday afternoon, eyes furrowed, hands clenched at her sides, marching with the grim determination of someone getting some unpleasant task finished so they can cross it off their to-do list.

This now seems to be the new normal, especially for parents. Whether toothpaste or school breaks, my wife and I do our best to avoid what we call "being overwhelmed by life." Not always, but most of the time we do avoid it, and for that, I have my mother to thank. Through her actions, every day she demonstrated that there is no need being overwhelmed and complaining about what you have to do in life since you have to do it anyway, whether you want to do it or not, whether you complain about it or not.

If anyone could have been overwhelmed by life, it could have been my mother. She had five kids, she worked, she led the uniform exchange at our school, and she did all the other things we modern parents get overwhelmed by. Also, did I mention that I'm a triplet? (The other two are girls, and no, we aren't identical, and no, we don't feel each other's pain.) And not only are we triplets, we are "Oops!" triplets. My parents had two children and thought their family was complete when ten years later they discovered Mom was pregnant. Surprise! And being 1980, when ultrasounds were far from common, they didn't find out until the end of the second trimester that their surprise baby was actually surprise *babies.*

According to my brother, despite all the shock and stress of having to take care of and provide for three more kids, Mom never complained. Dad, however, didn't handle the news quite so well. According to Delfino family folklore, my father spent the following three months in shock. He went to work, came home, ate dinner wordlessly, then he went to bed. But not Mom. She was firmly on the Triplet Train, which in the final trimester has only one destination. She was having these babies, so there was no use complaining or being overwhelmed. I'm sure she probably worried or wondered about what was going to happen, but she carried on with what she had to do.

And that is what she demonstrated for us as we grew up. I never remember her complaining about the endless cooking and laundry that comes with five kids. When we were babies, everything was done without ceremony or fuss. She always says that in order to avoid meals taking forever, she'd just line up our three high chairs and put food into the first open mouth. If one of us (I'm looking at you, Triplet #3) never opened her mouth, Mom didn't stress and try to feed us something different. There would be another meal in a few hours.

Mom continued to carry on resolutely even in emergencies, which were just something else that needed to be taken care of without complaint or someone (or everyone) freaking out. One emergency I remember clearly was when she sliced her hand open with electric gardening shears. We must've been four or five when it happened. My sisters and I were playing in the backyard, while Mom trimmed the large bushes along the back fence with classic 1980s, yellowish-tan electric shears. The trimmer was one that looked like two sets of saw-toothed shark noses that move back and forth, cutting everything in their path, whether leaf or my mother's hand, when it got too close. She said that after it happened, she looked down at the deep gash, which ran diagonally along her entire palm, and knew without a doctor telling her that she needed stitches.

My memory of the incident starts with Mom driving us to the doctor's office herself, her hand gripping a ball of gauze that steadily grew dark red as she leaned over our VW minivan's bus-like steering wheel. I don't remember her complaining or yelling at other drivers as she drove. (I wish I could say I drove as calmly as she did when something similar happened to me a few years ago.) To us kids, it seemed like she was driving us to our general practitioner's office as though we were getting our yearly check-ups. While she explained to the receptionist what happened, the three of us dashed for the built-in fish tank that fascinated us with both the fish and the fact that it was built into the wall. We watched the fish until Mom took us with her into an exam room to get stitches. In the one concession to her wound, she stopped for dinner at a fast food restaurant on the way home. Mom cut her hand, so we got chicken nuggets and fries for dinner. To us it was a great day!

My mom is still this way, which can be infuriating sometimes. She's survived breast cancer twice now and had both knees completely replaced. Most of the time I don't even hear about it from her at all. I'll call my parents, and Dad will casually mention, "Remember your mother's knee surgery is tomorrow."

"Uh, no one told me about that," I'll say.

"Well, you know how your mother is about these things," Dad will say vaguely.

When I talk to her again, I'll always complain, "Why didn't you tell me you were getting your other knee replaced?"

"Oh, don't worry about it," she'll say. "It had to happen, so why make a big deal about it? I'll be fine, and I didn't want you to worry since you've got all those beautiful babies to take care of. How are they doing?" (She's an expert at moving on in conversations by changing the subject.)

I never fully appreciated this trait of hers until I became a parent of four beautiful babies and noticed how overwhelmed so many of my fellow parents are these days. I try to remember not to worry about feeding kids, because you've got to do it whether you are overwhelmed or not. Don't worry about when baby walks or potty-trains or is thumb sucking, because, as Mom says, "No one has crawled down the wedding aisle in diapers."

So I learned from my mother not to waste energy or time being overwhelmed by life, since it keeps coming for you no matter what. Do what you have to do and keep going, even when frustrated and frazzled with something inherently crazy-making—like the toothpaste aisle. Ultimately, your choice of toothpaste isn't that important, so just pick one and get on with your life. After all, it isn't like you're having triplets. And even if you were, it's not that big of a deal. Just ask my mother.

Andrew S. Delfino is primarily a stay-at-home dad and humor blogger, who also teaches writing part-time to college students. After listening to his four kids have temper tantrums whenever he asks them to do something, he goes to work and listens to bigger kids have temper tantrums whenever he asks them to write something. While he doesn't mind being called an "asshole," he hates being asked if he's babysitting when he's out with his kids. You can read his parenting stories at: AlmostCoherentParent.com.

With You on My Side

By Tamara Bowman

Let it be known, my mom is funny. She tells fart jokes like the best of them. She once made up a game involving made-up disgusting stories about family members she didn't like. Mature? No. Hilarious, vivid, creative, sick-minded, slightly passive-aggressive, but oh, so wonderful? Yes!

She's also fantastic at Cards Against Humanity.

Did I mention how fiercely incredible she is? Or incredibly fierce? If you know me in person (or in social media life—which isn't so different in my case), you might think I'm nice. You might see me smile or hear me compliment your writing, your photography, or any number of things. You might know I'm on your side. All of this comes from my mom—a woman who will stop to help an elderly person cross the street, answer a phone call from a friend in need, and smile at twenty people she knows in public—all at the same time.

I call this "Emotional Multitasking."

It's the ability to be a lot of things for a lot of people. It's the ability to be a lot of things for a lot of people *at the same time*, because there's no other way. It's about spreading yourself too thin, but knowing no other way to be. You can't NOT answer that email, that text, or that phone call.

When I was around four years old, my world was shattered. I was having dinner with my mom and sister while my father napped. He got out of bed, collapsed onto the ground with a massive heart attack, and was wheeled out the front door, never to return home. My mom came home that night to retrieve us from the neighbor's house and had to tell us—her two daughters—what had happened. She had to call his parents and his siblings and his friends. She had to let people into her home and into our grief the very night after he passed away. Neighbors, family members, and friends came and went, but that night it was just the three of us in the house long after bedtime. We sprawled together in the big bed and became a team.

It hasn't changed.

I can't fathom the strength it took for my mother to go on, as she continued to raise us on her own. I'm sure it wasn't easy and wasn't without its share of impossible moments, but my mom knows how to make me feel like anything is possible. When she eventually remarried and moved us into my now-dad's house with three new siblings, she knew I needed my solitude and sleep and had a large room built for me in my own wing with my own bed. Still, I crawled into my sister's bunk bed nearly every night for years, but I liked knowing I had my options. I liked knowing I was being heard and considered.

When I was eight years old, I came home from school and told my mom I saw a leprechaun in my classroom. I didn't really see a leprechaun, unless you count the green construction paper one on the walls. I don't know why I told her this, but I imagine I needed to know she still heard me and that she was listening. I needed to remind myself I could say outlandish things to her, and she wouldn't freak out, abandon me, or tell me that I'm silly.

She never told me I was silly. In fact, she actually believed my leprechaun story!

In fourth grade, I had a mean teacher. She asked us to bring in insects for a science project and then she proceeded to drown them in water, in front of us, because they were too loud. She was so mean that I would cry in class. She would yell at me, only making me cry harder. I was so miserable that my mom stormed into the principal's office—a woman who was only ever known as calm and nice, but could kick up a real storm if need be. I was placed into another classroom right away, with the nicest and warmest teacher you could ever know.

I finally flourished that year, because my biggest supporter was always on my side. When I wasn't old enough or strong enough to have a voice outside of home, she became my voice.

When I was waitlisted at my dream college—Douglass College at Rutgers University—my mom said, "I still believe." She took me to meet with an admissions counselor and she said, "I still believe." I took my SATs and college placement exams, and I arranged an overnight orientation at another college where I'd been accepted. When I came home from the orientation in tears, because I didn't have the same passion I did for the other college, my mom said, "And yet, I still believe."

I took her words into my heart. I thought about her strength, her ferocity, and her love for me, and I wrote a letter to Douglass College, inviting them to rethink their decision to waitlist me—citing my high placement exam results and SAT scores. I ended my letter with, "I still believe, and I hope you do too." I got a letter from Douglass College only a week or two later that said they had decided to review my application again, at *my* request, and decided to accept me. I was officially Douglass material and a Douglass student. I screamed when I opened my letter and ran into my mom's arms. But we weren't surprised.

I have lived my adult life by her words, "I still believe." When the man of my dreams broke my heart, quite terribly, she stayed by my side overnight on my old twin bed. You know what she said, right? She said, "I still believe." When I was long over him and in love with another man, this heartbreaker came back into my life. My mom wasn't surprised at all.

I was surprised. Eventually, I got over my shock and married him. Her blessing meant the world.

When I was pregnant with my first child, my daughter, I pored over my mom's baby journals because I wanted to be everything she had (and has) been to me as a mother. Luckily, I didn't have to study hard because the ability has always been contained in my heart. Sure, I'm a different person—more callous in some ways and more wounded—but I think I have that same mothering heart.

The most important thing she's ever taught me is that she's always on my side. This has taught me how to always be on my kids' side. I'm not saying I don't sometimes tune my kids out or that the ferocity is always well formulated. When my daughter reported back to me that a little girl at school had asked her why she's so short at age five, I resisted telling my daughter to retort with, "Well, why does your face look like that?"

My mothering heart is imperfect, as everyone's heart is. Sometimes the best way you can be on their side is to step back, and let them figure out the solutions. Experience has taught me that this grows and grows as they do. I imagine that letting go never gets easier, but we can hope to get better at it over time.

I can't always step in with my witty retorts and my Mama Bear tendencies, but what I can do is truly hear my children. I can offer warm reception, open arms, and a deep knowledge of unconditional love. I can step back. I can give space—but if a teacher is drowning insects in front of them or a school or job isn't giving them the attention they deserve, you can bet I'll step in with the ferocity that was shown to be effective when I was a kid. I will show them kindness and fairness and how to fight for what they believe with kind, but firm words, and a never-ending belief in what we are all capable of accomplishing. I will always be *by* their side and *on* their side. I'll be that voice in their ears saying, "I still believe."

That is the gift my mom always gave to me, and she still does every day.

Tamara Bowman is a mama of two, a professional photographer, a writer/blogger, and a professional cookie taster. She has been known to be all four at all hours of the day and night. She is a very proud contributor to the book *The Mother of All Meltdowns*. After two cross-country moves, due to her intense Bi-Coastal Disorder, she lives with her husband, daughter, son, and slew of strange pets in glorious western Massachusetts. Visit tamaracamera.com or themotherofallmeltdowns.com.

Lessons from a Working Mom

By Brooke Takhar

When you're a kid, you don't catch all the subtle parenting moves that are happening around you. Maybe you can't. Like if you looked too hard for them they would leap just out of frame; flickering firefly moments that zip just out of your grubby, outstretched fingers.

So you're just a kid and you carry on with your Fruit Roll-Ups and rolling your jeans just right, until suddenly you're getting married and having a kid and you're *so* tired and have *no* business raising and curating a life.

You go back to work—you *have* to go back to work—and your plate groans with responsibility and regret.

You're guilt-ridden, scrambling, and worried about everything you do, say, and feel as a parent, holding a hand that you made, but just for a precious few hours of the day.

You pause though, in a moment of calm reflection that side-swipes and surprises you. You realize every instinct you have as a parent is coming from a small seed tucked behind your heart that grew as you *yourself* were parented.

When I look back on my childhood, my mom and her seemingly casual grace raising two kids by herself, I see now she gave me the map for being a working mom. It's a careening course with no brakes, but lots of room for detours and improvisation.

Here are just a few breadcrumbs she left for me to find and devour:

Don't Return Anything Under Fifty Dollars

"MoooooOOOOooom, my new ___ is broken!"

"How much was it?"

"I don't know, maybe fifteen dollars?"

"We'll buy you a new one."

I never stood in returns or a customer service line with my mom. She had no time. Well, she had time, but she wasn't about to spend it waiting to argue with a customer service rep. Sure, this lead to a lot of our stuffed garbage bags dotting the landfills, but we helped the economy too.

Pay People to Help You

I'm guessing, on average, my mom had about nine hours of free time Monday through Friday. She didn't want to spend a hot second of that vacuuming or dusting around our ridiculous toy mounds. So she hired a housekeeper to come in once a week and do a good once-over along with a few loads of laundry. *Brilliant, right?* That meant the times she was home with us, she could just eat dinner and hang out with us while we snuggled like newborn puppies in her lap.

Don't Stress Over Baked Goods

If Pinterest had been around in the 1980s, my mom still would not have been sucked into the hype. I never once ate a sweet baked good from our oven, and I was still happy and husky and eventually super resourceful. For example, if you wrap a Rainbow Chips Ahoy cookie in a paper towel and nuke it for ten seconds, it becomes four hot, buttery bites. *Better* than homemade.

Enable and Trust Your Kids

When I was eleven and my brother was six, we finished our long stint of attending a home daycare. We were deemed responsible enough to walk to school by ourselves, an hour each way. When I was eleven and a half, I learned how to iron, how to carefully chop chicken into stir-fry chunks, and how to pack our lunches. Afterward, my brother and I roamed our neighborhood in the summer, popping into the air-conditioned video store to rent movies and using the change to fill small baggies with sugary, gritty 7-Eleven candies.

At thirteen I learned how to drive a standard, first in mom's work parking lot, cranking the wheel and us around the small buildings, and then eventually down a long dead end country road, carefully easing from first to second gear with no grind. My brother and I were responsible enough to feed the dog and cats. We bathed ourselves. We got stuck and asked for help, and were shown how to do it. Any mess we made or mistake we fumbled through, we figured out a solution. Instead of snatching away the messy hard parts, our mom walked us through them so we could own them and feel powerful and useful and helpful. The three of us in that red bungalow on Marine Drive were a team, but she let us lead. The pride beamed out of our eyes like spotlights.

Keep Your Kids on Their Toes

Every time we were taken out for dinner, the meal ended with a similar refrain of, "This is the *last* time I'm taking you guys out." So you could say that was a classic parenting fail using this baseless threat. But we really *did* feel bad and would each promise-whimper we would be better next time. There was just *something* about a restaurant booth that made me and my brother turn into competitive weasels, kicking under the table, reaching for the same forks and then duelling with them, up-ending water jugs all over our table, and soaking our paper placemat drawings and colorful napkins. The quintessential disastrous meal we all remember is when she put her fork down, stood up, grabbed her purse, and marched to the car. My brother and I sat there mute, eyes huge and darting over at the server, staring at each other with a silent, "WHAT DO WE DO NOW?"

We knew then that our mom wasn't the predictable beast we'd learned to take advantage of. She could surprise us at the worst times and that knowledge was tucked away and remembered forever.

Give Your Kids a Taste of the Exotic

A week in Disneyland. A month backpacking in Scotland, Ireland, and England. A bed and breakfast on Galliano Island. The Four Seasons Hotel in Seattle for Christmas. These were all expensive vacations, well out of our budget. They were few and far between, giant peaks that dot my childhood, meant to increase my thirst for more, more, more. **We could've gone on more trips within our means, within our province's vast backyard.** We could've camped, stayed in godforsaken motels in towns we didn't care about. My mom had only a certain amount of vacation time, and she didn't waste it on halfway-mediocre experiences. We were never bored when we went away because it was all foreign and magical and cool, and we felt deep in our little bodies how special every second was.

Work Hard

To this day, when I call in sick I think, "MY MOM WILL BE SO DISAPPOINTED IN ME." I believe that over her thirty-plus years of work, she has only missed one and a half days ever, and that was when her mother passed away in a quiet, gray hospice.

Growing up, when mom was at work, we couldn't call her unless it was a limb-dangling emergency. She was busy. She was doing important things. Work was the fourth member of our family that stole her away, but we knew that her work supported our tiny family. We let work have her until the sun hid, and we'd wait and listen for the snarl of her tires on the gravel drive and leap out at her, desperate to show off our new Lego creation and choreography to "Neutron Dance."

Work swallowed her days, but we understood she was needed and she needed it, and so we shared her with her work and grew up to gently fear but tremendously respect this concept.

Now *I* am the working mom. The daughter became a mother. I walk in her shoes, but with a greater support system and the benefit of the lessons I learned growing up.

I'm easier on myself. I may not be the voice my daughter hears all day, but we are joined by an invisible rope as we get through our days—separate but together.

I know now, based on experience, that no matter how many kind villagers help raise you and walk you through all the steps of your life, when it matters, you only ever want your mom. And when it matters, she will always be there. It's true for me, and it will be true for my daughter.

My tight shoulders settle back softly into place when I nibble on this thought.

They say we all eventually become our mothers, and I see it in the mirror clearly now, hear her cadence come out of my lips, and marvel at how my handwriting loops in the same lines as hers. I'm supposed to shudder at the thought, I know. But if you are lucky to have a mom like mine, who juggled a career, her life, and her children like bright balls of fire in the sky and never dropped them, not even once, you'd be okay with it too.

Brooke Takhar is a Vancouver-based storyteller and mama of one goon. She runs so she can eat ice cream and blogs so she can make fun of her parenting mistakes. If you need a pen pal, gluten free recipe, or a meaningless celebrity gossip partner, she's your gal. You can find all her exaggerations at *missteenussr.com*, her personal website for the past sixty-five years. Brooke's stories have also been featured on *BLUNTmoms*, *Scary Mommy*, *In the Powder Room*, *Project Underblog*, and *Review 2 a Kill*. When she's not writing, sleeping, or dumping black coffee into her corneas, she co-hosts a podcast with her brother called *I'm Right & You're Wrong*. Spoiler alert—she's always right.

Just Ask: Questioning My Mother and the World

By Jen Simon

When I was seven, I wanted to be an artist, a doctor, a writer, a judge, a mermaid, and "like a virgin" when I grew up. Of course, I didn't know what a virgin was, but Madonna made being one sound so exciting. Oh yeah, and I wanted to be Madonna too.

My mom watched me make up dance routines and sing my off-key heart out to inappropriately wonderful songs. She bought me jelly bracelets and sundry cheap-o items to emulate Madonna's look. And when I asked her what a virgin was, she told me in an age-appropriate way.

While they loved her, my mom's parents weren't talkative; they weren't open or very accessible emotionally. Unsatisfied and left wanting more, my mom decided even before she had children that she would be a different kind of parent. She wanted to talk to her children. She wanted her children to feel comfortable coming to her no matter the subject—sex, drugs—

it was never too daunting, embarrassing, or inappropriate. And growing up, my mom impressed upon my sister and me that she would answer any question we had. *Just ask*, my mom told us—*just ask*.

This was before the Internet of course; before we carried the answers to nearly all of the universe's questions in our pockets. But who needed the Internet when you had an all-knowing mom?

When I wanted to know what a virgin was, of course I asked. When everyone at Sunday school was titling about "69," I knew enough not to plead ignorance to my friends. I knew who would explain what it was without laughing at me or rolling her eyes. Of course, I was horrified and weirded out when she told me, because why would adults want to DO that? But at least I knew the answer.

When my mom got her period and began puberty, her mother gave her books. End of story, no discussion. The books would explain everything. My mother also gave me books, but as a prelude to conversations. They were a jumping off point from which to ask questions. I laughed at the ridiculous drawings of chubby, animated naked men and women. I stared at their wild curls in strange places. But it helped with the basics and Mom filled in the rest. No question about sex or maturing was too risqué or off-limits. When I asked about tampons, she even showed me how to put one in!

Just ask—my mom repeated throughout my childhood and teenage years. If you don't ask, you will get no answers. If you don't know something, *just ask*. If you have a question, *just ask*. If you have a problem with something going on, *just ask*. The lesson to ask didn't end at my mother. It has reverberated through my life, expanding my world.

My mom taught me to be a feminist before I knew the meaning of the word. My body was my own. I was to respect and value it, but also to use it as I saw fit. As long as I was confident in my choices, I could contemplate why society's norms were well, *the norm*, and reject it if I chose to. When I went through my rainbow-hued hair phase, she gave me old towels to use and told me not to ruin the grout in the bathroom. When I started piercing things, she disapproved but knew that the decision wasn't hers to make.

Just like my body was my own, so were my thoughts and my choices. And if someone told me no, I had a response: why? If you have a rule, you better have a reason for it, because if I don't agree with you, I will ask. I will ask why. I will ask why not. When you have no fear of asking, your life becomes open-ended. It becomes rich with possibilities.

Throughout my life, I've never stopped asking. Whether it was a teacher, a boyfriend, a boss, a salesclerk, if I have a question or need something, I'll ask. I'm not intimidated. I will not assume things will work themselves out or just turn out okay. I know that if I don't stand up for myself, and be my own advocate, no one else will.

Because I learned to ask, I also learned to tell. Because she taught me about sex, I told my mom when I lost my virginity. Because she talked to me about smoking, I told her when I tried it. I talk to my mom nearly every day, sometimes several times a day. We're incredibly close, because I know I can trust her. I know I can ask her anything, or tell her anything, and I do. Some people might think it's strange, but my mom knows my secrets. Some of the things I tell her disappoint her, but regardless of what I say, she loves me, and I know there's nothing I can tell her or ask her that will change that.

I've been extraordinarily lucky to have a mom who, above all, only wanted (and wants) the best for my sister and me. She has dedicated her life to us, teaching us innumerable lessons about ourselves, parenting, life, and the world around us. But by far, the most important lesson was to speak up for ourselves and for what we believe in. And to ask when something seems wrong, strange, or just confusing.

Now that I'm a mother, I'm trying to raise my sons in a similar fashion. I want to cultivate the same kind of honest, trusting, back-and-forth with them that I have with my own mom.

While they will probably go to my husband with questions about puberty (and I certainly won't show them how to use a tampon), I want them to know they can come to me with questions big and small. Sometimes I get a little help from Google for my five-year-old's space questions (Jupiter is the biggest planet, it turns out), but I'm happy he asks. I hope there are many more questions in our future. And I hope that he and his baby brother will always know I'm available for them—all they need to do is *just ask*.

Jen Simon writes for many publications including *Huffington Post, Babble, Scary Mommy, Lifetime Moms,* and more. She has contributed to four anthologies. She stays home with her sons—a toddler and a sleep-challenged five-year-old. You can follow her on Facebook at facebook.com/jen.simon1.

My Mother's Voice

By Ramona Scarborough

My mother had unique ways of teaching me morals. When I was about ten years old, my mother and I were walking down a city street, when a large, burly man came toward us. When the man was out of earshot, she asked, "Did you see what that man was doing?"

"Yes," I said. "He was smoking a cigarette."

"Do you know smokers suck on their cigarettes, much like a baby with a pacifier?"

I began to laugh, picturing the macho guy with a baby binky in his mouth.

As a teenager, I couldn't see cigarette smoking as sophisticated or desirable, because of the image my mother had planted in my mind.

She chose an attractive lady spewing out vomit over a railing to teach me why excessive drinking is "not all fun."

Once, when I lied about something, she said, "Do you want your life to be difficult or easier?"

"Easier," I said, sighing, knowing she had me again.

"When you tell the truth, you never have to cover yourself or remember who you told what. Your conscience won't pinch you like new shoes. Lying is like digging a hole, which gets deeper and deeper, and finally, you can't get out. No one will trust you, and trust is the basis for loving relationships."

I never had a problem with stealing, but I remember she warned me not to steal the limelight.

"Let other people shine, listen, and applaud. It's one of the secrets to being well liked."

She wanted me to get acquainted with older people too.

"What do I say?" I asked.

"Ask them about childhood, things they enjoyed doing, where they came from. Don't ask about their health or you may be there all day; it's usually negative. Tell them about yourself. What you're learning in school or about your cat, things like that. When you leave, ask them if they would like a hug, they might miss being touched." I ended up having so many adopted grandmas and grandpas and enough stories to fill several books.

On another occasion, my mother encouraged me to reach out to those with difficulties. A man with muscular dystrophy sat in a wheelchair, on the side of the road, waiting with us for the stoplight to change. My mother greeted him in a friendly manner, ignoring the fact that he was drooling and swinging his head back and forth. She waited for him to finish speaking and offered to push him across the street. I felt frightened of the man and tried not to look at him. Again, after he waved good-bye, she turned to me.

"Do you realize that could be us tomorrow? We don't know when an illness like that can strike us. You need to think how you'd like to be treated. Would you like to be ignored or treated like everyone else?"

My life has been greatly enriched by this advice. People with disabilities—the blind, deaf, or intellectually disabled—have been welcomed guests at our home, and they became my friends.

Mom also made a point of stopping to talk to people who did caretaking for relatives, children, or friends.

"You're my hero," she'd say to them.

To me, what she was saying was, "Can you imagine the efforts of the caregiver, who sees to their needs day after day, for years, feeding them, cleaning up after them, bathing them? Hardly anyone notices them—even the person being cared for often can't express their gratitude. She makes a sacrifice every day."

She inspired me to do a little "window dressing," as she called it, keeping myself dressed up nicely on the outside. She also drew my attention to women who had improved themselves on the inside; charming women, intelligent women, those who helped others.

"Later in life, these traits will be your best assets."

She told me once, "If you keep trying new things, you aren't old." I've never quit doing new things, even when I've been scared.

Another habit she ingrained in me is a special gift. "Look at the sky every day, it's never the same. Stop your hurry for a few moments."

However, here's the main reason she told me to do this: "If you think you're really something, compare yourself to the sky. You are a small speck in the universe."

Two days before my mom died of a stroke at age ninety-two, she lost her ability to speak. She said, "I love you," in the way she squeezed my hand. She said, "Thank you," when she smiled, while I brushed her hair and gently washed her face. When I sang some of the old songs we'd always sung together, I saw her tears and understood every word she said.

My mother, Anna Miller, has been gone many years, but her voice is in my head and heart, and I still listen.

Ramona Scarborough hopes her mom's advice has made her into a moral, charming, intelligent woman she would've been proud of. Her mom probably would've been surprised to find her life story written in Ramona's second published novel, *Anna's Diary*. Ramona wishes her mom could've known about the stories she's written, which fulfilled a childhood dream of becoming an author.

Children Should Be Seen, Not Heard

By Nancy White

Some life lessons are harder to learn than others. You know the easy ones. Don't touch the stove, it's hot. Never run with scissors in your hand or a lollipop in your mouth. Wipe your feet before entering the house. Other lessons challenged my reasoning ability, and I consider myself of average intelligence.

Like the time I kicked little Henry in the balls when I was eight, because I was playing horsey, and he got in the way of my stallion rearing up. It must have been a hefty kick, because his parents sued mine. It turned out that little Henry may not have been able to reproduce in the future.

My parents tried to explain to me that I should avoid kicking boys between their legs from now on. I didn't understand, of course. I was on the playground, and Henry walked into a rearing stallion. Any idiot knows better than to do that. You get the idea of what my parents had to deal with. How could I be at fault when I hadn't done anything wrong?

I need to back my story up a couple years here, because the beginning of what I learned from my mother began when I was six. My education began at a military dinner club in Tokyo, Japan. Being the oldest of four children, and the only redhead in the family, strangers were always asking my mother where the *redhead* came from. She replied the same way every time.

"From the milkman." Then she and the inquiring party would laugh. She never said it in front of my father, but I think that was because he was a military man and on duty all the time.

On that Sunday evening, in the Tokyo dinner club with my whole family, we waited to be seated. The doors opened and a couple entered. A soldier came right up to me and tousled my red curls. "Hello, sweetie, where did you get that red hair?" He gifted me with a broad smile.

Before my mother could answer, I spoke up, "From the milkman." And then I laughed like Mom always did. There was a long moment of silence. At the time, of course, I had no idea the magnitude of embarrassment this caused my parents. Looking back on it, I guess that was a pretty risqué innuendo from a six-year-old.

My mother gasped, holding her hand over her mouth, the blood draining from her face. "Nancy, why would you say such a thing?"

"That's what you always say, Mom."

My father wished the soldier and his wife a pleasant evening, as we moved to be seated. I had the feeling I'd said the wrong thing. But how could I have? I told the truth, didn't I?

That night while being tucked into bed, my parents sat with me and explained that my red hair came from an Irish grandfather. I also had an uncle with red hair. They stressed that if anyone should ask in the future where my red hair came from I was to respond, "From my grandfather." I pointed out that's not what Mom says. Daddy assured me that Mom would say that from now on.

A few months later, with Christmas season upon us, our family spent a Saturday putting up the Christmas tree and decorating the house. The banister needed a fake bough of pine needles draped up its length. I asked if I could do it, and my mom gave me little finishing nails and a hammer. She showed me how to do the first one and went back to decorating the tree. One would think there was no way I could screw this up. And one would be wrong. I tried to nail the tiny, little nail into the banister railing and missed the nail, hitting my thumb instead.

What happened next is what always happens when someone hits their thumb with a hammer. I threw the hammer to the floor and yelled, "Shit!" All jolly activity in the room froze, as five sets of eyes turned toward me. I knew instantly that I was in deep you-know-what again, but had no idea why. My mother climbed down off the stepping stool, the one she was using to put the star at the top of the tree, and advanced toward me.

"What did you say, young lady?"

"I said, 'Shit,' Mom. Is there something wrong with it?"

She explained that I had used a curse word and only grownups say curse words and then only when necessary. I was forbidden to say curse words from that day forward. Well, the short and the long of it was, I got my mouth washed out with soap. Let me tell you the taste of soap stays with you for a while. My appetite was off for a couple of days.

Since the pine bough event, my mom never had to ask me if I was listening to her. Every time she lost her temper, for some reason or another, and let a curse word escape her lips, the same question from me was her reward, "Was that necessary, Mom?"

I managed to control my runaway mouth for a few years. By then we had been transferred stateside and were living in Arkansas. If memory serves me right, that summer was blistering-the-paint-off-the-siding hot. Base housing did not include air conditioning. To save money, Mom would wash, starch, and iron Dad's uniforms herself. As with everything else in the military, the creases on a uniform had exact mathematical requirements. We're not talking about ironing your basic tablecloth here. Press one crease a millimeter off and it went back into the washer. On one particular ironing day, a neighbor lady came up to the fence and asked me if my mom was home. Born absent a bashful gene and a natural tendency to tell it as it is, I replied, "She's in the house drinking beer, smoking cigarettes, and ironing."

The neighbor blanched and looked aghast. I guess in 1960 this categorized Mom in the "fallen woman" category, but I'm not sure. Again, clueless to my gaffe, I went back to playing with my sister. The neighbor went up to the porch and knocked on the door. Soon I noticed Mom on the porch thanking the neighbor for stopping by and wishing her well. The next thing I knew my mother stormed out the back door, grabbed me by the arm, and jerked me into the house. This time my penance for telling the truth was a paddling.

"Well, Miss Motor Mouth, I guess you'll think twice before you gossip about your mother again, won't you?" Her face was crimson with anger. I was blubbering.

"What did I do wrong, Mom?" Clueless, that's my life.

"You know what you did, young lady. You can't go around the neighborhood telling people that your mother is in the house smoking and drinking. What are the neighbors going to think?" So that neighbor lady must have told Mom what I had said, and Mom didn't like it. *Why?*

I must take after my dad because her logic made as much sense to me as savoring the last slice of her homemade chocolate cake in front of my siblings. Why should we care what the neighbors think? Let them think whatever they want to think.

"But, Mom, you were in the house smoking and drinking. I didn't lie." That logic earned me a slap in the face. Clueless. Again.

What I learned from my mother was that the truth doesn't always set you free. Sometimes the truth comes with consequences. I went to Sunday school every Sunday morning before attending mass. "Thou shalt not bear false witness against thy neighbor." That was ingrained in me since before I could remember. I was one of those people who believed if you treated others fairly, they would reciprocate. Although this is generally true, I was being set up for a rude awakening.

I learned the hard way that milkmen do not leave physical attributes in a milk bottle to be doled out to hapless children. I also learned that certain words in the English language are set aside for a pre-determined age group, but are not publicized as such in the hope that you will get your mouth washed out with soap, like your parent before you.

Little Henry missed six weeks of school because he had to have an operation and probably never had children. I'm sorry, Henry. I didn't mean to hurt you. My parents lost the lawsuit. Sorry, Mom and Dad. Even when you're using your imagination and playing alone, as we used to do back in the old days, you're still responsible for those you hurt in the real world. And, if your mom is in the house without air-conditioning, watching soap operas on a blistering hot August day wearing short shorts and a halter top, trying to place in the precision ironing marathon competition, do not fault the woman for having an ice-cold beer and a cigarette. This only presents her with the opportunity to teach you a new skill.

That day she taught me how to iron my dad's uniforms. If I didn't do it right, it went back in the washer and I had to do it over. I was allowed ice water, but no snacks because they would leave grease on the uniform. I could watch soap operas, however, because my mom watched while relaxing on the sofa, enjoying a cigarette, and drinking an ice-cold beer. At least the truth set her free. I love you, Mom. Rest in peace.

Nancy White is a freelance writer and member of the Scribophile Critique Group online. Her craft memberships include Romance Writers of America, Central Ohio Fiction Writers, Women Writing the West, and The Writer's Center. Nancy has two previously published memoir short stories: "The Boss from Hell" in *Work Literary Magazine* and "You're Safer on a Plane Than in a Car" in *Shatter the Looking Glass Magazine*. Currently she is working on her first historical western novel.

Fuchsia Lipstick

By Marlynne Powell

It was September, 1988, and the first day of school. I was starting eighth grade at a junior high near Hollywood, and I really only cared about three things:

If I should cover my science textbook with the new *Tiger Beat* magazine pull-out poster of New Kids on the Block, or if I should cover it with my *Right On!* magazine poster of Jody Watley.

1. If I could convince my parents to buy me a coat, like the one Janet Jackson wore in her "Rhythm Nation" video.
2. And, most importantly, showing off my hot colorful lips, wearing the first tube of lipstick I ever bought—a Wet n' Wild's fuchsia-colored shade that said, "I'm like totally cool to the max!"

This was a significant and even somewhat rebellious action, since I wasn't allowed to wear makeup. But I'd used some of my money from doing chores to sneak and buy the tube from the local drugstore so I could be one of the "radical chicks" in school, along with my "totally awesome dudettes."

On the first day, I remember my mom dropping me off, giving me a kiss on the cheek, and telling me not to forget the lunch she made for me, right before I jetted out of the car eager to see all of my "homegirls" that I had missed over the summer. I ran into the arms of my best friend, Charity, unable to wait to show her the tube of lipstick that I'd hidden inside the plastic red pencil case in my backpack—complete with New Kids on the Block and Kirk Cameron stickers plastered on the outside. We laughed all the way to the bathroom just before the first period bell rang and smeared it all over our lips. We had no clue how light or heavy the lipstick should be applied. All we knew was that we were going to be the most bitchin' girls that our eighth grade class ever saw! And we were!

Throughout the morning, in between each class period leading up to lunchtime, I must have shared that tube of fuchsia lipstick with every single one of the girls in my crew. After seeing the color all over my sandwich, my bottle of orange juice, and imprinted on my apple and graham crackers, I just had to apply another coat.

I was so excited about wearing the lipstick, and passing it from friend-to-friend, that by the time school let out, I felt utterly "fantabulous" walking around the grounds. So fantabulous that I'd forgotten to wipe my face clean in the bathroom before hopping right into the front seat of my mom's car when she picked me up after school.

My mother gasped when she looked at me. I instantly developed a huge lump in my throat. *Oh, no,* I thought. *I'm in big trouble.* But instead of the reprimand I expected, complete with a "You're on punishment, young lady" speech, she just shook her head and laughed before blurting out, "We've gotta do something about that *ugly* lipstick!"

I let out a sigh of relief and laughed along with her before replying, "Well, everybody at school thought it was cool, so ..."

"And just who is *everybody?*" she asked.

"You know ... all my homegirls in my clique."

She nodded and smiled. In hindsight, I think she was happy that I had a group of girlfriends; many of them were the same girls I'd hung out with since seventh grade. She was a fifth grade teacher, and she knew how hard and sometimes cruel girls could be toward one another, especially as they approached and experienced adolescence. So while I was glad she reacted that way, I was still scared.

When we got home, I was sure she'd tell my dad that I wore lipstick to school, but to my surprise she didn't. After dinner and homework, while my dad watched Monday night football, my mom called me into her room and had me sit in her vanity chair. I stared into the lighted mirror.

"We're going to do something different tonight," she started. "We're going to try on makeup."

I was giddy and couldn't believe it! "Are you serious?" I questioned. "But I thought you and Dad had a 'no makeup until high school' policy?"

She just shrugged her shoulders and said, "No, that was *your dad's* policy. Now remember, this is our little secret, okay?"

I grinned from ear-to-ear. Not because we were doing something behind my dad's back, but because it felt like she finally saw me as something more than her "little girl."

"But I have a few rules to this makeup policy change," she began, while staring at my reflection in the mirror and stroking my long, dark-brown hair. "No ugly black eyeliner, no mascara, no eye shadow. *Just* lipstick. Got it?"

I nodded in agreement, when truthfully, I didn't even know what eyeliner was, and I definitely had no interest in mascara. To an eighth grader, it looked like it might hurt to put on! All I wanted—and my righteous homegirls—was lipstick.

My mom started by handing me a red tube. I struggled to put it on properly, so she showed me that you had to start with tracing the tube around your top lip line and work it around before adding a quick swipe to the bottom lip. "And watch those mouth corners," she advised. "The goal is to have the lipstick slightly accentuate your face, not to have it look like a frosted cake."

I took her suggestion seriously while she watched on. But it didn't matter. We both looked in the mirror and blurted out, "No way!" It was too dark and way too sticky.

"No worries," my mom told me. "Every color won't be for you. With lipstick it's kind of like trial and error."

I smiled, while wiping my lips with the soft tissue, because she was right. And because she seemed like she really wanted me to test out all the colors, even if they didn't exactly work for my more tan skin tone compared to hers, which was fairer.

"Here, try this one," she stated, while handing me another tube. This one was a peachy-coral tone. I took my time putting it on, pressing my lips together to smudge properly as she'd suggested. We both in agreement yelped, "No!" It was much too bright and dry on my lips.

We followed that one up with pink lipstick, laughing out loud at how silly it made me look. I started to feel like a "fashionista" Goldilocks—every color was too "this" or "not enough that." But that didn't matter. In between trying on lipstick colors, we talked about school, what I liked about eighth grade, how it was different from seventh grade, and what I appreciated about my homegirls. We even got to whether there was some boy that I had a crush on. Of course, I "kept it real" and told her that I was going to either marry Joey from New Kids on the Block or Ralph, the lead singer of New Edition, so any boy that liked me would have to take a back seat to them.

Interestingly, since she was a teacher, I realized that it was also *her* first day of school. She talked about some of the kids in her fifth grade class—which kids she thought were really smart, which students she might have to pay extra attention to, and even the students that made her laugh. She gave me advice about making sure that I chose my homegirls by the way they treated me; not by hoping they'd like me because I was sharing my lipstick with them. And I gave her advice, too, about making sure that the kids in her class, who might struggle with their assignments, be given enough time to complete their tasks and maybe even offer them tutoring afterschool. She agreed.

We bonded about our shared first day of school. It was probably the first time I felt like I was having a "grown up" discussion with my mom, and it was fun since we were testing out lipstick colors the whole time.

After trying on a bevy of horrible colors that made us laugh out loud, my mom handed me a mocha shade, and just like Goldilocks eventually recognized, we both excitedly exclaimed in unison, "This is just right!"

We hugged. She told me I could keep the tube of lipstick. I ran to my room and placed it in my backpack, ditching the fuchsia color for good.

Now that I'm approaching forty, I share this story because—to no one's surprise—going to department store makeup counters and checking out the sales, at places like Sephora and Ulta, is one of the activities that my mom and I love to do together. We try on lipsticks and perfume and during these times we discuss our lives—what we're looking forward to and what we're glad is ending. It's during these times that we get a chance to share advice, just like we did all those years ago on the first day of eighth grade.

I appreciate my mother and all that she has done for me, especially all the advice she has given me about growing into a woman, about being a mom, about having a career, about just anything and everything. But the one bit of advice that stands out the most is being proud and happy about who I am no matter what obstacles life may bring—and, of course, about staying away from that "gag me with a spoon" 1980s fuchsia-colored lipstick!

Marlynne "Marley" Powell is a freelance writer, a prose author in several genres, and an all-around lover of anything that involves pen-to-paper. She is an accomplished grant proposal, academic journal, and magazine article writer and has published articles in *Non-Profit World Magazine, The Next American City, Planning and Zoning News Journal,* and *The American Planning Association New Planner,* among others. She is passionate for writing flash fiction, humorous short stories, and travel writing. You can visit her at marleywrites.blogspot.com and festiveaffordablevacations.wordpress.com.

Just Be Yourself

By Lee Morris Williams

"Just be your unique self, there's no other human being on earth exactly like you. That makes *you* special," became my mother's mantra when we eight children were growing up. She repeated it so often we switched channels, like we did when she watched Lawrence Welk's *Dance Party*.

I never realized what a special lady my mother was until I took her on a Mediterranean cruise for her seventy-fifth birthday. Well, perhaps there were fleeting moments of appreciation, but because she was so provincial and had never traveled more than a hundred miles from home, my siblings and I were mostly embarrassed by her, especially her plain dresses, no makeup, and that Pentecostal hairdo.

In 1985, I scheduled a Mediterranean cruise for us aboard the luxury cruise liner, *The Golden Odyssey*, to visit Greece, the Greek Islands, Egypt, Turkey, and Israel. Mom had always been a religious woman and her lifelong dream of visiting the *Holy Land* was finally coming true.

"Mom, if you could travel anywhere in the world, where would you go?" I knew what her answer would be, for I'd heard it many times.

She stopped loading the dishwasher and turned around. "I'd visit the *Holy Land*. Going there has been my lifelong dream. You know that. But I guess it wasn't God's will or He'd have let me go. Anyway, I've had a long and happy life. You know, many of my friends never made it to seventy-five."

"Well, guess what, Mom. God and I have decided to grant your fondest wish for your birthday." I handed her a packet containing our passports, tickets, and a brochure describing our Mediterranean cruise aboard *The Golden Odyssey*.

"You've got to stop teasing me this way, Lee."

"No, Mom, I'm serious. Look at the tickets. Whose names are on them?"

"Well, they say ... oh my goodness! *Our* names are on them!" She sank onto the chair and spread everything on the wooden table. With an open mouth and eyes wide, she gazed up at me in disbelief. She then bit the side of her forefinger, and tears came to her blue eyes and cascaded down her wrinkled cheeks. She put her palms together and lowered her face like she might be praying. Raising her face toward the ceiling, she mouthed the words, *thank you, God*. Then, she grabbed me, squeezing until I could hardly breathe.

On our flight from Nashville to New York, Mom was like a child who'd never been anywhere. Wide-eyed and curious, she kept busy conversing with fellow passengers. "What's your name? Where are you from? Where are you going? How many children do you have? I'm the mother of eight children, and I've never traveled before. We're going to the *Holy Land* where

Christ was born." Most passengers were friendly and kind, but some frowned or stared in silence.

"Now, Mom, when we get to New York you must not talk to strangers," I said. "They're not as friendly as we Southerners are. You have to be cautious."

"Well, maybe I could teach them to be friendly. Most people are nice, you know."

"But not everyone is. Just promise you'll not talk to everybody you see."

"Oh, Robbie Lee, you are so suspicious of people."

"Please, Mom, and just call me Lee, not Robbie Lee."

"But that's your name. You're not ashamed of your name, are you?"

"Robbie Lee sounds so southern. We won't be seeing many Southerners. Promise, Mom, just try to observe and listen. You're going to see and hear so much on this trip."

"I thought this is supposed to be a fun trip. How can you have fun if you can't talk?"

"Please, Mom," I begged. She just rolled her eyes and rushed toward the lavatory. I saw her talking to a flight attendant on the way. He patted her arm and smiled.

In New York's baggage claim area, as I retrieved Mom's bag from the carousel, I saw her follow a woman around talking to her like a long lost friend. Then she trailed beside a young woman and child until they were out of sight. I rushed through a maze of travelers until I overtook her, led her back to our area, and ordered her to sit on her suitcase until I could spot the remainder of our luggage. She sat there, but continued welcoming passengers to New York City.

On the New York to Athens flight, Mom met an Austin, Texas doctor and his wife sitting across from us and a couple of university professors from Hawaii seated behind us. Upon learning that both couples would be on our cruise, Mom again began her inquisition. In five hours, she learned more personal details than I could have acquired in five years.

We boarded ship in Athens and were led to our stateroom by a young Greek god who asked if he could go back to America to serve as our chef. "I eat out most of the time," I said. "I'm not sure I could afford you."

"Then let me go back and be your pool boy."

"We don't even have a pool." I said. A look of disappointment spread across his face as he led us into a small suite with fresh flowers, a bowl of fruit, and a bottle of Greek wine waiting.

Mom had exited to the small balcony and was communicating with the Greek taxi drivers blowing kisses from the shore. "I think they're flirting with me," she said, blowing a few kisses of her own.

"Mom, they're taxi drivers hoping to get the rich Americans' dollars."

"And I thought they just liked us."

At dinner we were assigned a table with six other passengers, including the Hawaiian professors, an Argentine artist and her attorney husband, and two single ladies from California. Enjoying our Greek gyros, broiled lobster and shrimp, and baklava, we listened as our dining mates discussed their travels, yachts, planes, homes, luxury automobiles, and family jewels. For the first time since we left home, Mom seemed speechless. She had not yet uttered a word beyond the introductions.

"Well, Mrs. Franks, you're awfully quiet. Tell us about your family jewels," said the corpulent lawyer.

Mom squirmed in her seat and looked questioningly toward me. I shrugged and extended my upturned palms. I'd never seen my mother at such a loss for words. After a prolonged silence, with everyone staring in our direction, Mom straightened her narrow shoulders, stuck out her chest, and said in a small voice, "I'm the mother of eight children. They're my family jewels."

Everyone applauded, except the Hawaiian couple. They turned around in their seats, seeming to search for someone across the crowded room. "Way to go, Mrs. Franks," said the lawyer.

The next night, cruising through the Greek Islands of Mykonos, Skaithos, and Rhodes, we dressed for a masquerade party. Mom and I had no costumes, so I made her a cape from a lace tablecloth I'd purchased in Athens and a tiara fashioned from a plastic ice bucket. I dubbed her Czarina Irina. I cut off a pink candy-striped cotton dress to about four inches above my knees, purchased a giant-sized lollipop from the ship's gift shop, made me some Mary Jane shoes from high heels, and went as Shirley Temple.

Czarina Irina and Shirley Temple sat at the bar drinking ginger ale as the passengers danced to Greek folk music. Everyone in costume had to go onstage and introduce themselves. "I can't do that," said Mom. "I'd be scared to death."

"Just be yourself, Mom. Isn't that what you always taught me?"

Most costumes were elaborate and professional. The fat lawyer dressed as Adam and his artist wife was Eve. The Hawaiian couple portrayed pirates. The doctor and his wife dressed as a doctor and nurse. The California women went as Lady Godiva and Jackie Kennedy. One couple dressed as Queen Elizabeth and Prince Phillip.

When it was Mom's time to introduce herself she bounded upon the stage and stood there speechless. Everyone laughed. I wanted to disappear. The emcee asked, "And who are you, little lady, and where are you from?" and stuck the microphone in her face. She soon grabbed the mike like she knew exactly what to do. "I'm Czarina Irina from Iuka." She passed the microphone back to the emcee.

"Where the hell is I- U-Ka? That sounds like a Greek burp to me." The audience roared.

"Iuka, Mississippi," said Mom.

"Miss-sip-pi?" That sounds like my kindergarten teacher," said the man in his Greek English. "Where the hell is Miss-sip-pi?"

"In the good old USA," said Mom. "You know, the home of Eudora Welty and William Faulkner. I bet you've never heard of them either."

The crowd cheered. Then they gave Mom a standing ovation. She beamed like the Star of David. The audience chanted, *Czarina Irina, Czarina Irina, from Iuka, Mississippi, Iuka, Mississippi, USA! USA!* The emcee handed the mike to Mom, threw up his arms, and left the stage. Someone from the audience yelled, "Tell us about your family jewels, Czarina."

Mom stood erect and said into the mike, "I'm the mother of eight children." The crowd roared. Mom stood there smiling until someone escorted her off stage. When they announced the winner of the contest as *Czarina Irina*, Mom practically ran across the stage to accept her trophy, a statue of Diana.

The next day, as we docked at the foot of the volcanic island of Santorini with its sparkling white buildings with royal blue domed roofs, a loudspeaker announced our arrival and explained that the English translation of Santorini was Saint Irene. The Texas doctor asked Mom if the island was named for her. Mom turned to me and asked, "Do you think that's possible, Robbie Lee?"

"Mom, anything is possible in the Greek Isles."

At Israel's Port Haifa, Mom got so excited she doubled over with chest pains. I thought she was having a heart attack.

The doctor from Texas rushed over, examined her pulse, asked someone to get a wet cloth, which he put on her forehead, and ordered her to lie still. Passengers encircled her awaiting a diagnosis.

"Long live Czarina Irina!" proclaimed Dr. Prescott as he stood and extended his hand to help Mom up. "She'll live to be a hundred. She has the heart of Methuselah. She's just suffering from exhilaration."

That night we learned that the Hawaiian professors had asked to be seated at another table. They said they wanted "more interesting and intellectual conversation than that stupid Southern woman could offer." I don't know if they meant Mom or me.

At Jerusalem's Wailing Wall, we met a petite Palestinian bearded man who hugged Mom and said in broken English, "Welcome to God's country! We love Americans. We just don't like your leaders."

"We feel the same way sometimes," said Mom, as she returned his embrace.

As we marched up the Via Dolorosa, Mom turned to me and asked, "Can't you just feel the presence of the Lord here?"

I gazed into all the gift shop windows at the cheap trinkets, postcards, and visitor guides. *It looks like Disneyland to me*, I thought, but didn't dare say it aloud, for fear of spoiling Mom's reverence.

Inside Bethlehem's Church of the Nativity, Mom gently touched the Tomb of Jesus and prayed a long, silent prayer. Then she rushed over to me and hugged me so hard it hurt. "Do you have any idea how much I love you, Robbie Lee?"

On the way to the Church's gift shop, Mom and I strolled past a security guard with a *Moses* nametag. He shook our hands and asked where we were from. Mom said, "This is

Robbie Lee and I'm Irina. We're from the USA and are sailing on *The Golden Odyssey.* I'm the mother of eight children, and I'm having a glorious time." *I guess she had forgotten her real name.* Moses hugged us both much too long and finally let us move on.

I bought Mom a plastic crucifix and a small Jesus of Nazareth statuette. When I reached into my purse for money to pay, all my cash was missing. I searched and searched, but found nothing. I turned to see if Moses could help, but alas, he was nowhere in sight. I asked the clerk where the guard went and she replied, "Which guard? We don't have a guard." That's when I realized I'd been robbed of four hundred dollars. Thirteen loose dollars was all the cash I had left. Thank goodness Moses didn't find my passport and credit cards hidden in my pantyhose.

After dipping small bottles of Holy Water from the River Jordan, and watching the sun set over the Mount of Olives, we took our bus back to The Golden Odyssey.

Later, with a guide named Abraham, who we watched like a hawk, Mom and I strolled along the same marble streets that St. John and St. Paul had walked in Ephesus (now Kusadasi, Turkey). We visited the ancient city of Constantinople (now Istanbul), rode camels around the Great Pyramid and Sphinx near Cairo, Egypt, and ate lunch at the Hilton Hotel overlooking the Nile River.

For the remainder of the cruise, every time Mom met someone new, she would stand erect and declare, "I'm the mother of eight children! They're my family jewels."

Back in Iuka, Mom became the family jewel. Even though she fractured a hip nine years later and suffered dementia from poor circulation, she remained an inspiration for her family and friends.

Mom moved herself into Tishomingo Manor Nursing Home, which she alternately referred to as her home or her hotel. She obviously adopted the entire staff and residents, for she claimed them all as her children. One day, rocking on the front porch, she said, "Why don't we just buy this place? It's big enough for our whole family."

Mom's golden odyssey through life continued. Most days she could be seen ambling along Tishomingo Manor's corridors on a walker or racing along in her wheelchair sporting a first-place blue ribbon she had recently won in a basketball-shooting contest. Some days you could hear Mom serenading the residents with "Amazing Grace." Or you might spot her in the lobby greeting guests with her cheery "Hello" or waving "Bye, ya'll come back soon!"

All she had to do was just be her unique self. That's what made her so special.

Lee Morris Williams is an artist, writer, and photographer who writes both fiction and nonfiction. Her first, still unpublished novel won a coveted BreadLoaf Writer's Conference Contributorship Award. Two of her short stories won a regional award for a University of Memphis free semester's workshop conducted by the acclaimed author, Richard Bausch. She has also written newspaper and magazine articles, two short story collections, and a philosophy eBook called *Search*. Lee loves learning, and her grandchildren accuse her of attending college for forty years. Lee has owned daycare centers, modeling schools, a health and fitness spa, sold and appraised real estate, developed, conducted and emceed national seminars, hosted two cable television talk shows, served as a higher-education administrator and consultant, and taught school from kindergarten through college. Lee is married to Dr. Roy H. Williams, Jr. They have six children, twenty-two grandchildren, and ten great-grandchildren. Lee also has six sisters and a brother.

All in Good Timing

By Lisa Romeo

My mother would have turned ninety next year, in time for her to see my eldest son graduate college. She herself had to leave school at thirteen to work in a factory. That she died four years ago, two weeks prior to his high school graduation, particularly rankles, because she abhorred bad timing.

She never quoted the worn out saying "timing is everything," but believed in a more nuanced, personal timing, gleaned from a life hewn sharp and clear during early difficult days.

In 1947, she was two months pregnant when she married my father. In their conservative, Italian-American, Roman Catholic families, the timing couldn't have been worse. Yes, they'd been dating exclusively for five years and had been engaged for a year. But my father's moderately well-off parents, who owned a business, a house, and rental property, were already upset with his choice of fiancé, the daughter of a poor, illiterate, on-the-dole mother who'd been abandoned by a husband with a second secret family.

"So, did you time that?" I once asked her when I was in college. "Did you figure if you were pregnant they'd have to accept you?"

"No, that was an accident. Bad timing," she assured me. "And they never let me forget it." My father never wavered, she said. And I never did the math until I was fifteen. But by then they had three children (I'm the youngest), and when my father died, they'd been married fifty-nine (mostly) happy years.

What she had to teach me about timing, and what I learned when I needed to, however, had more to do with timing what we *can* control.

Infatuated with horses, practically before I could talk, my pleas for a pony from age ten to thirteen only made my father smirk. (*Are you crazy? Where would we put a pony? Do you think I'm made of money?*). But Mom was on my side and knew of a stable nearby, one that we could afford. Winking, she told me to drop it for a while. So I started asking for a dog instead—which both opposed. (*No animals inside the house, period!*)

Then I signed up for a summer acting camp, one my father had found and supposedly vetted, one that cost a bundle and ended up as a bust. I left, along with dozens of kids, on the first day. The parents all wound up in small claims court in September. But I arrived home downtrodden, a vacant summer sprawling ahead.

That first night home, while eating out, I asked for a dog again. Both said no, but when my father went to the men's room, Mom leaned in.

"Now," she said. "Ask for a horse now. The timing is just right."

One horse turned into five, and then into ten years on the horse show circuit, and on to blue ribbons, with my parents both beaming from the bleachers.

When I was twenty-four and my on-again, off-again boyfriend—the boy I'd been infatuated with at age twelve, the teenager who dumped me at fifteen and then disappeared for eight years, the man I was in love with but who couldn't commit—was now alternately making me dizzy with love or miserable with heartache. I sat with my mother in her new Las Vegas living room over Christmas break. Frank was twenty-seven-hundred miles away, and I wondered what to do when I got back.

"Should I fish or cut bait?" I moaned.

"Do you think he's the one?"

"I do."

"Then it's all about timing," she said, sitting up straighter. "When he comes swimming around again, you reel him all the way back in, and then, just when he's firmly on the hook, toss him back."

"What? And what if he doesn't come back?" I protested. "It's 1985! We don't play games like that anymore."

"Well, *he's* playing. And he's got the timing down so well, that as soon as you're in deep, he'll jump ship. Turn the tables. Time it just right, you'll see."

I fished. I reeled him in. But when I should've tossed him back, I instead timed a simple "Three strikes you're out" notice for an evening after I'd cooked his favorite meal. We married three years later on Mother's Day.

As a son-in-law, Mom liked Frank immediately. He shared her sense of timing: flowers when I wasn't expecting them, surprise tickets to Bermuda when my job stress reached a zenith, and for twenty-one years, always offering, "You fly out and visit, I'll handle the kids," each time either parent needed me.

Two years after my father died (during my first semester of graduate school), my mother, who at eighty was still bowling, playing slot machines, and traveling, suffered her first heart attack (three months before my grad school graduation). "Sorry kid, lousy timing," she said shortly after my plane landed in Vegas.

I stayed for two weeks. The night before I left, sensing her anger at her situation—old, widowed, frustrated at being slowed down—I walked her to the oversized garage, now half empty. I picked up two empty one-liter seltzer bottles from the recycling bin, and threw them at the closed garage door.

"Any time you're mad, just throw some bottles," I suggested.

A one-time softball pitcher, she liked the idea. Weeks later, after her doctor told her traveling might not be a good idea, she felt the time was right to hurl some bottles.

"I threw them as hard as I could," she said. "I felt a little better."

A month later, she flew to my sister's home in Massachusetts, and a week after that, they drove to Maine for my graduation. I asked how she'd gotten her cardiologist's consent.

"He said all my numbers were good, my heart was healed, and I should enjoy life and do what I want," she explained. "It seemed a good time to say what I wanted was to see you graduate."

Lisa Romeo's nonfiction, journalism, poetry, and reviews appear in mainstream and literary print and online venues including *The New York Times, O-The Oprah Magazine, Babble, Under the Sun, and Literary Mama.* Her work has been nominated for Best American Essays. She lives in New Jersey, teaches in an MFA program, and works as an editor, ghostwriter, and writing coach. Her blog, *Lisa Romeo Writes*, features author interviews, writing craft advice, and resources.

What Matters Most

By Tracy Sano

I love my mom. I really do. You should hear how her voice lights up when I call.

"HEY, TRAAAAAACCCCYYY!" She always makes me feel like a celebrity is calling or something.

Maybe it's because I don't call her enough, but that's not the point. Whenever I come home for visits, Mom gives me THE BIGGEST hugs, like rib-crushing-so-happy-to-see-me hugs. Again, maybe because I don't visit enough. Again, not the point.

Mom's Christmas packages are bar-none. She always remembers the littlest things that I like, even if I've forgotten that I like them. She'll send things like Swedish Fish or a pair of pink slippers, because I mentioned in passing I needed a new pair—and let's not forget Snoopy. There's always some kind of Snoopy involved.

When I was born, my aunt brought me a little Snoopy stuffed animal to the hospital. From that day forward, Snoopy and I were inseparable. I called him "my doggie" and dragged him around with me everywhere. I think back to the countless meltdowns I had had after getting home from a restaurant and realizing at bedtime that I had carelessly left Doggie in a booth. My parents would trek back to retrieve him until we finally decided it was best to leave Doggie at home—bless their hearts.

Mom is so funny. She collects all kinds of Snoopy paraphernalia all year round for my Christmas package, because she thinks I still love Snoopy. Every year I shake my head laughing, as I pull out some random Snoopy ornament or T-shirt. But if you want the truth, I'd be sad and disappointed if she stopped sending them. So I guess in a way, I do still love Snoopy.

My mom and I couldn't be more different. For starters, growing up she'd wanted to have twelve kids and to live on a farm. As long as I can remember, I've been terrified of animals, and making me live on a farm would be a cruel punishment comparable to no other horrendous thing I can imagine.

When we were kids, Mom would take us to the mall, and as we'd pass by the pet store, my siblings would run in and pet the rabbits, puppies, gerbils, or whatever pet happened to be on display in the center of the store. All the little kids would be gathered around, eager to get their hands on those filthy varmints. Sometimes I'd pretend to be brave, and I'd stick my hand into the glass box, covered in dirty woodchips and rabbit poop. Before my hand got anywhere close to one of those little things, I'd imagine it biting off my fingers with one of its sharp teeth or catch a glimpse of one of their beady eyes and freak out, yanking my hand back with a gasp.

After a few of those anxiety-filled trips, I stopped fooling myself. Instead, when we approached the pet store, I'd sulk back, asking my mom for the pennies out of her purse. Then I'd sneak over to the wishing pool outside of the store and toss the pennies in one by one, making the same wishes over and over. *Please let the pet store go out of business. Please let rabbits become extinct.*

As for the twelve kids, Mom ended up only having four kids. (Underachiever!) She said it was because after she had me, she realized she didn't want to go through childbirth that many more times. I think it was a lie. I think she would have kept going, but Dad probably told her they couldn't afford it and put his foot down.

As for me, I've never wanted kids. At one point, I contemplated adoption, because I thought I might be a pretty cool mom, so I mapped out a plan to adopt a little girl.

When my niece was born, my sister Mandy got all over me about it.

"When are you going to adopt your little baby? Kailee needs a cousin, and I want to raise our kids together!"

"Okay, Mandy, but we still have time. I mean, if we want them to be the same age, I don't plan on adopting her until she's like five or something ... you know, that way she'll be potty-trained and can talk and stuff. Or maybe six or seven, since then she'll be in school and can help me with chores ... or maybe I'll adopt a teenager. Yeah, a teenager seems like more the age I can handle. We'll scoop up an eighteen-year-old. Well, shoot, if she's eighteen, we might as well wait until she's twenty-one so she can have a glass of wine with me and go out with the girls ..."

As I sat seriously pondering, I looked up at Mandy, who was staring at me with wide eyes, and with her mouth gaping open.

"What?" I asked, innocently.

"What the hell is wrong with you? Do you want a kid or a friend?"

Look, I love my sister's kids and my cousin's kids. I actually enjoy spending time with my friends' and families' kids. But I would never, ever willingly expose myself to spending any period of time with a stranger's kids.

Mom, on the other hand, LOVES little kids. She doesn't care whose kids they are, but the littler the better. I don't think she really knows how to deal with them once they get older than around eight, which would explain the timing of the birth of my youngest brother, Bobby, who is seven and a half years younger than I am. "Bring in the replacement kid!" I used to imagine her yelling, like the director on a movie set. Kind of like on the Cosby Show when Rudy got too old and they had to bring in Olivia for cute-kid-factor.

The day we brought Bobby home from the hospital, I was the "new Rudy." (Only paler and I didn't have a friend named Buuuud.) Mom stayed home with us until we were all in school. Then she got a job at a school working with little kids. She loved those little kids and tried to tell me stories about them. She was so enthusiastic about what little Johnny did on the playground or that Sarah did something super funny during story time. I had no idea how to respond to those anecdotes, which usually surfaced when I was in the middle of telling her something really serious.

"Mom, I'm just devastated. Eric and I broke up this week, and I can't stop crying. What if I didn't do the right thing?"

"Oh, Tracy! That reminds me ... last week during arts and crafts this little boy, Eric, made the funniest picture and ..."

"Mom. Just put Dad on the phone, please."

Usually those conversations led me to drink heavily—which brings me to another difference between my mother and me: she doesn't drink. Like, ever. Meanwhile, I threaten to check myself into Betty Ford at least once a year, after I've gone on a particularly bad bender. When asked what my hobbies and interests are, typically the first answer that comes to mind is "drinking wine" followed by "writing short stories, while drinking wine," or "organizing and attending bottomless mimosa brunches," and "happy hour," not necessarily in that order.

Mom doesn't generally keep any alcohol in the house. Okay, wait! I have stumbled upon a similarity! I don't keep any alcohol in the house either, because I keep it in my stomach, after I've consumed every last drop. To her credit, Mom does recognize that some people like to drink, so when she has a family gathering at her house she makes sure to stock up on some tasty alcoholic beverages for the "drinkers."

One time when I was home for such an event that warranted supplying booze, I went shopping with her for my brother's high school graduation party. On her list was "beer and wine."

Go, Mom! I was so impressed.

As we filled up the cart, Mom made a pit stop down the beer aisle and threw in a thirty-pack of Budweiser. Then she got a determined look on her face and began scouring the shelves. After a few minutes, I couldn't resist.

"Ma, what are you looking for?"

"I'm trying to find those good wine coolers. You know, the berry ones I always get. I don't see them anywhere."

I didn't know what to laugh at first: that she called wine coolers "good" or that she said the ones she "always gets." I've seen my mother drink a total of ten drops of alcohol in my entire life, and I'm pretty sure nine of those drops were from a Zima bottle. But let's not split hairs.

Fighting a fit of laughter, I sputtered, "Mumma, you can't find them because they stopped making wine coolers in 1989!"

But Mom was determined and four supermarkets later, she had located a store that carried her berry wine coolers and bought two four-packs of the foil covered bottles that she "always gets."

When we got home, I helped her put the groceries away and asked to borrow her car.

"Where are you going?" she asked.

"To the liquor store, Mom. To buy the kind I always get."

"Okay! But when you get back maybe we could split a wine cooler?"

Later that week, when we were getting ready for the party, Mom called me into her room, and asked me what she should wear. Happy to help, I stood in her closet and surveyed the options. As I rummaged around, I found a hodgepodge of outrageousness almost impossible to describe. I discovered everything from 1980's blazers, complete with large buttons and shoulder pads, to leopard-print MC Hammer pants, and sweaters she had pilfered from my closet—ones I had left behind when I had moved. I stumbled upon turtlenecks in every color of the rainbow, flower-print dresses, and sparkly jackets.

Upon my quick inspection of her shoe collection, I discovered a pair of hideous black, sneaker-style shoes that I immediately recognized as those that had been issued to me when I waitressed in college. I had refused to wear them, citing the reason as: too repulsive to let my feet touch. My manager had said, "Tracy, you have to wear them for safety reasons! They are non-slip for when you're in the kitchen." I told her she could fire me if she wanted, but I wouldn't be wearing those shoes, and I'd sign a waiver saying I wouldn't sue them if I slipped and died while on the clock—because should I die, I would not be caught dead wearing them.

"MOM! Why do you have these shoes in here? I thought I threw these away like eight years ago! Tell me you don't wear them in public?"

Indignantly, Mom grabbed the shoes from my hands and placed them back in their spot in the rack. "I do wear them. They're comfortable," she stressed. I could not have been more horrified.

My love affair with shoes has been a long-lived one. My closet has always been jam packed with shoes. When I was getting ready to move to California from New Hampshire after college, I don't think anybody really thought I was doing it until they witnessed me purging my shoe collection.

"You're really moving, aren't you? I wasn't sure until I saw you giving away shoes! This is really happening!" My dad had said.

Whether they're heels, wedges, or boots—the perfect shoe can complete an outfit. I've got shoes every color of the rainbow, prints, peep-toes, booties, and even shoes with bows and embellishments. I love designer shoes, but always appreciate a bargain find too.

As I get older, I can understand wanting to wear comfortable shoes, but even my flats have to be fashionable. My mother would never understand how much I love shoes. That was obvious since she was willingly hanging onto those old orthopedic shoes from my waitressing days.

Our differences don't stop there. Mom loves doing crafts and is happier than a pig in shit come the holidays when she gets to invite her friends over for gingerbread house-making parties. Sometimes I feel disconnected from my mom, not only because you couldn't pay me to sit around and make a gingerbread man, but while I'm constantly checking my three email accounts, Facebook, LinkedIn, Pinterest, Instagram, Twitter, and text messages on my phone, Mom doesn't use the cell phone that we bought her unless it's "an emergency." I'm not really sure what constitutes "an emergency," or even a good time to use her phone, in her mind though.

One time she was supposed to pick me up from the airport. She told me to call the house and she would leave, so that by the time I got my bags I would only have to wait a little bit. I suggested that I could just call her cell phone like a normal person, but she informed me that she couldn't because it wasn't an emergency.

Every once in a while Mom will call me from her home phone. When she does, it's usually at 7:00 a.m. on a Saturday or when I'm at work. If she doesn't catch me, she leaves me a message, "Trace? Oh. This is Mom. I have a message for you. So call me back so I can give you the message." I don't know HOW many times I have to tell her that voicemail is used to GIVE THE MESSAGE, not just to tell me that she has one. How would she like it if I wrote her a letter and told her to mail me a letter back so I could mail her one with the information? She doesn't think that's the same thing, she tells me.

And don't even get me started about her and emailing. She deletes them—all of them! Her reasoning, "Well, Tracy, I don't check my email a lot so when I do, I just don't have time to read them all. I just have to delete them." Yes, yes, Mom, that makes perfect sense.

Even though my mom can be ridiculous, and even though we don't have a lot in common, I look back on special moments, like at the grocery store hunting for "good" wine coolers together or us fighting over those god-awful shoes. My mom has taught me that we don't have to like the same things to like each other. My mother's bone-crushing hugs and Snoopy Christmas packages, her excitement when I call—those are the things that matter.

My mother has taught me that our shared love for each other is more important than a shared love for shoes—even hideous black orthopedic ones. Ma, seriously, I love you, but please ditch those damn shoes!

Tracy Sano has always loved telling funny stories. Her humor blog, *Tracy on the Rocks*, was a 2015 finalist for "Best Writing" and a 2014 finalist for "Most Humorous Weblog" in the popular "Bloggies" Awards. She is a contributor to the anthology *I Still Just Want to Pee Alone* and has been published on *Scary Mommy, Mamalode,* and featured on *BlogHer* multiple times. Tracy has an unhealthy obsession with firefighters, hot dogs, and anything pink. Her favorite thing to do-besides drink wine is to laugh until her stomach hurts (which doesn't take much, considering how much she also hates working out). She resides in San Diego, and her biggest accomplishment to date is being named World's Best Auntie

I'll Never Look Like That

By Catherine MacKenzie

My mother has taught me many things over the years, some of which I had forgotten and I'm now re-discovering at the age of sixty-three. Ideas I had thought were mine actually came from her.

I am now an adult—older than an adult actually—I've been a mother, and I'm now a grandmother. I never thought I'd age into a grandmother.

One day when I was a pre-teen out riding my bicycle, I noticed my maternal grandmother standing in front of the bedroom window, her sagging breasts hanging down toward her waist. *I'll never look like that*, I promised myself, looking down at my then flat chest.

As a teenager, I'd stare at my thirty-five-year-old mother and think how ancient she appeared and how I would never grow *that* old. Today, I'm past the age I thought I'd ever reach. Where did the years go? How did I arrive *here* this fast? Sometimes I think my best years are gone, with too few years left to accomplish so many things I suddenly want to do, wishing I knew then what I know now, especially when I look down to see a grandmother's gravity-fed breasts.

My mother lives over two thousand kilometers from my home. I'm not a phone person, but I do call her on occasion. Most times, however, I just email. I probably should telephone her more, but email is more convenient in my busy life. She doesn't seem to mind—at least she's never vocalized any displeasure; she knows I'm here for her and vice versa.

When I recently asked my mother to jog my memory with reminders of what she had taught me over the years, she provided me with a list. She did say that most of what she had written she actually couldn't remember teaching me or my siblings, but she figured she *must* have taught us all of those things and more. My mother also shared that surely I must have taught my own children those things as well, which of course I had.

Most of what I learned from my mother are lessons that all mothers teach their children. Didn't every mother tell her child not to leave the house without wearing clean underwear? Or, "Eat all your dinner. Don't you know there are starving children in China?" I never could understand that one! If I didn't eat my food, how did the children of China benefit? And the usual admonitions: respect your elders; do your homework; be nice to your siblings; always tell the truth; be kind to others; bathe regularly; and brush your teeth before bed. My mother also told me and my four siblings to stand up straight and tall. I still think of those words today when I find myself slouching.

Two things my mother neglected to include on her list were strength and independence. I never realized how strong my mother was until my father died. She relied on my father during their forty-nine-year marriage, as the breadwinner and her best friend. After my father's funeral, my mother, who was an only child, collapsed outside their bedroom door and wailed that she was an orphan. Her parents were deceased and her husband was gone too. There was no one left but her five children. We had our own lives. But my mother picked herself up and carried on.

My maternal grandmother, who had lived in a basement apartment in my parents' house for many years, was very dependent upon them until her death. My father found it difficult having her there. My mother learned from her mother's clinginess and adamantly stated she would never be a burden on her children. Now in her mid-eighties, she lives an independent, full life.

Another thing my mother said she had taught me was to save my money. Perhaps I would be a multi-millionaire had I remembered that one! She also told me to take care of my toys and books. I'm passionate about my books. In fact, I still have some of my childhood books, so I don't doubt she did tell me this. My nagging to my children and grandchildren about the care of their toys and books must have come from my mother, although my words are on deaf ears.

We were taught to say goodnight and kiss our parents before bedtime. As a teenager, I quickly weaned myself from this routine after strolling into my parents' bedroom one night to catch my father lying in bed in a state of undress. I'm not sure if my parents noticed when I quit the habit, but nothing was ever said.

I remember my mother rising at the crack of dawn on Thanksgiving and Christmas mornings to prepare the turkey. When I was a newlywed, I used to get up extra early too.

Now I awake at my usual time, and my turkey is still ready. I still follow my mother's food traditions at these times of year, especially her stuffing, candied sweet potatoes, mashed potatoes, and canned peas.

At Easter, my mother would spread a paste of shortening and dry mustard over what was to become a baked ham, then insert spiced cloves into the grooves she had cut. Maraschino cherries were placed in the center of the pineapple slices before it went in the oven. She also baked a pineapple upside-down cake, perhaps to use the leftover pineapple slices. I have done the same for years.

Friends comment on my quirk of covering my drinking glass with a napkin. I do it because no matter how many glasses are out there, it would always be my drink the fly finds and drowns in. I routinely offer everyone a napkin for the same preventative measure, but no one ever takes up the offer. It hit me a while ago that this was a habit of my mother's and a habit my young granddaughters have picked up since. Another ritual of my mother's that I follow is to drop an ice cube (or two) in a glass of white wine. And, thanks to my mother, cocktail hour begins at 4:00 p.m. in my household. *It's always four o'clock somewhere, right?*

My mother taught me to sew, an interest my only sister had no desire for. I hand-stitched before I was six, making clothing for my many dolls. Over time, I graduated to my mother's Singer sewing machine and fashioned my own clothes. Eventually I was given my own machine. My mother still remembers the day I called her to my bedroom when my machine quit working. After unscrewing the panel from the side of the machine, we found the belt in shreds from overuse. I ran that machine to the ground, the continual whir of the motor emanating from the confines of my bedroom. Unfortunately, my only daughter has no desire to sew; although, she has recently taken up knitting and crocheting, something else my mother had taught me. My daughter, however, taught herself and surprised me one day when she showed me various items she had crafted. I hope my granddaughters will start knitting, crocheting, and sewing at an early age, like I did, instead of waiting until their mid-thirties like my daughter.

Although my mother was a proficient seamstress, like her own mother, and could construct anything at the sewing machine, she had never done such work as cross-stitching, needlework, or macramé. I was her teacher in those instances.

I have, on occasion, glanced at myself in a mirror when I've passed by, sometimes catching a glimpse of my mother's face. No one would say I look like my mother, so I don't know why I see her there.

"Like mother, like daughter." *Isn't that the expression?*

Catherine MacKenzie escapes from her mundane world by writing poems and short fiction. Although she writes all genres, she often veers toward the dark and death, composing fiction most women can relate to. Cathy has been published in various print and online publications. She has also self-published several poetry and short-story collections. She also paints, pastels being her favorite medium, and her grandchildren are her favorite subjects. She lives with her husband in Halifax, Nova Scotia. Visit Cathy at Writingwicket. wordpress.com.

Open-Road Soul

By Chelsea Grieve

"We're lost. You're driving the wrong way."

I say these words as my mom navigates through the rural countryside of Nova Scotia. I'm in the passenger seat squinting at the map she bought at a gas station and glancing up to check road signs when they appear. I'm as irritated as only a child can be irritated, regardless of the fact I'm an adult with a newly granted M.A., which *should* mean I'm mature, right? But there is absolutely *nothing* like traveling with your mom to bring out your worse characteristics, and I'm actively choosing to forget the meaning of the word *mature* right now.

Mom takes a puff of her cigarette and flicks ash out the open window. "No, we're not lost."

My mom is decisive in her declaration. Since this is only the beginning of our exchange, she is also cheerful. She is absolutely convinced we're going the right direction and I'm overreacting, just as I'm equally convinced we're going in the wrong direction and she's underreacting. This is a typical conversation between the two of us. In fact, we had a very similar "discussion" while walking back to our bed and breakfast in Halifax the night before.

We pass another road sign, and I consult the map again. I do so as dramatically as possible, silently trying to communicate my frustration even though I know she's quite aware of my growing agitation. The sides of the map crinkle, and she proceeds to light another cigarette, half out of habit and half because her grown child is annoying.

"*Yes*, we are! That road we just passed is well past the one we *should* have taken!"

"I would know if we were going in the wrong direction, Chelsea."

"No, you wouldn't. Because we are *going* in the *wrong* direction right *now!*"

As the passenger, I can't do a damn thing. I throw the map down and fold my arms across my chest. I know I'm acting like a five-year-old, but she simply isn't listening. Strangely, this is the act that moves her from irritation to anger. From here, it's all downhill. We bicker until we eventually find the highway, leading us back toward New Brunswick and consequently, Maine. In a few days I'll be glad to leave Maine and move forward with my life as a post-grad, but right now I'm itching to get *back* to Maine. Mom continues to smoke, which pisses me off further, only making both of us even bitchier for the remainder of our time in Nova Scotia.

Luckily Nova Scotia is small, and everything is fine again once we reach New Brunswick. We laugh. I rub it in I was correct, she ignores me while lighting another cigarette, and we stop at Subway for lunch. It's all rather anti-climactic, but the proverbial storm has passed.

In many ways Mom and I have quite different, and sometimes clashing, personalities. I'm by far more social, academically inclined, and passionate about issues surrounding social justice. Sometimes I'm intense and overwhelming in my passion. My mom possesses more hermit-esque characteristics and is incredibly laid back with a general philosophy of *laissez-faire*. She believes in living her life as she will live it, regardless of what society thinks. On this platform we are well-matched. I'm simply more likely to become actively involved in social politics.

As you can imagine, our conflicting personalities often result in disagreements surrounding mundane, every day, beautiful life scenarios—like getting lost in Nova Scotia—that end up in laughter and teasing.

This is our relationship, and it's one many don't understand. We often sound like we're fighting, but we're not. Most of the time, arguing is like an endearment that sounds really, really mean to outsiders. If she doesn't want to talk on the phone, I accuse her of no longer loving me. She always says something along the lines of, "You're right. I don't love you anymore. Talk to you tomorrow." We aren't malicious; rather, it's a teasing ritual. I know she loves me, and she knows I love her.

At the end of the day, she gifted me with a very special kind of strength. It's the kind of strength in a woman that often intimidates others. It is the strength to be who I am and say, "Screw you," to the rest of the world, by living my life completely on my terms, with my values and moral compass as a (sometimes faulty) guide. Through her, I learned I'm worth more than forcing myself to change for the sake of others.

I learned by observation, and I watched my mom without ever knowing I watched. I never realized how every time someone criticized me, or my mom's parenting style, she would light a cigarette and very often say nothing at all. She simply ignored those who dared to criticize and moved forward doing whatever she damn well pleased. Was it always the right choice? No. I watched her make mistakes. But she owned her decisions, good and bad. I have found this to be a rare quality in adults, and because I lived with her, I can hardly suffer those who don't take responsibility for their own actions.

Character flaws and all, I am special. I don't say that out of vanity. I say that because to my mom I am special. Sometimes I'm a special kind of neurotic—like when she doesn't listen to my superior sense of direction—and sometimes I'm special simply because I'm Chelsea. Because she has never sought to change or control me, I know I have the right to be me in a world where I'm constantly judged for my body, intellect, relationship status, politics, sexuality, and social views.

Without her guidance, determination, and strength, my reality would look very different. Like every other young woman who doesn't conform, I spend a lot of time hearing that I'm not good enough. It's difficult, even if you know and don't agree with those values, and unfortunately, I've seen many of my own generation hear that very message from their own parents. There can be a lot of pain in trying and failing to be who the people you love claim you *should* be. I am lucky because I have nothing to hide from my mom.

I'm strong because she taught me to be strong; I'm independent because she taught me to be independent; and I'm comfortable in my skin because she taught me to be comfortable in my skin.

At the end of the day, when we're together—which isn't very often anymore—I don't need to think about who I am. I know who I am, and I know my mom isn't going to question that or suddenly hate me for my flaws. I'm safe, and there is something beautiful about knowing this is our foundation.

Chelsea Grieve spends her time writing and drinking copious amounts of coffee and tea. When she isn't writing, she works with non-profits, reads multiple books at one time, tries to belly dance, and explores the world of vegetarian cooking. Haku and Momo, ninja cats extraordinaire, accompany her on literary and writing adventures.

The Right Way to Fold Towels

By Elaine Alguire

I open the door to the clothes dryer, and the scent of clean towels overtakes me. I happily breathe it in. They are warm to the touch, and I grab one and pull it to my nose to inhale the scent vehemently. I pile them into the basket and carry them to my bed—folding them one by one. Some for our bathroom, some for the children's linen closet, some for the kitchen drawer.

My mother taught me how to fold bath towels many years ago. After she showed me her way of doing it, and I adopted her technique, I assumed there was no other way.

"Here, Elaine, watch. First you fold it in half, just so. Then, you fold one side over to the center and then again. Perfect, see?"

I could see in her face how proud she was of her towel-folding, and I wondered if her mother taught her too. I think she was proud, because she has always liked things clean and tidy. But I think she was also full of pride, because she had a nice home with clean towels that she could wash in a washing machine whenever she wanted. Growing up poor and on a farm will probably make you feel that way.

"Now you try."

In my first few attempts the towels came out a little crooked, but I quickly got the hang of it. I took pride in my skills as I sauntered down our hallway to put them away, my hands full of clean, beautifully folded towels ready for the family to use.

When I left for college, and was solely in charge of my own towel laundering and folding, I continued to do it that way. Again, it was the only way I knew. One of my roommates did it differently. She folded them in half and then only in half again, leaving huge towels to go in her small cabinet in our apartment. I showed her how I folded my towels and she said, "Yeah, I know. I have seen how you fold them. Too much work."

A few years later, I married. After living together for a bit, the towel-folding came up between me and my helpful husband as we stood together over a basket of clean ones. I watched as he started and finished one of the towels we had received for our wedding.

"You're doing it wrong," I said. It was my household now, and I wanted all my towels to be folded correctly, just as I had been taught. He was also in the fold-in-half-and-then-half-again camp, and I just could not agree. *How could I be married to someone who didn't fold his towels correctly? Why hadn't we discussed this before a date was set?* I teased.

He promptly refused to fold towels anymore. One of his favorite sayings is, "You can tell someone *to* do something, but not *how* to do it." I tend to disagree (especially in this particular area), but we compromised. I told him that it was fine and that I was happy to do our family towel-folding henceforth.

But then a baby came along, and laundry became quite the task. I asked him to help again, and told him that I did not give a lick how he folded the towels, as long as they were clean. There were times when I pulled them straight from the dryer to my body right out of the shower. Towel-folding techniques were the last thing on my mind after several nights of interrupted sleep. But out of habit, whenever I was in charge, I folded them my preferred way.

During a family beach trip with some of our good friends one summer, I was called out again for the way I folded my towels. The husband of the couple thought my way was too complicated. I told him it was the way I had always done it. Sure, there was the half-and-half way, but that was not my way. He insisted I convert, because it was so easy to just grab it out of the cabinet and suddenly have it unfolded, ready to dry off. I agreed that his logic made sense, but explained that I liked the way the towels looked better the way I chose to fold them.

I lay in bed one day while my mother was staying with us, helping out when my daughter was just a few days old. I was so grateful that she stayed with us for a week or so after all my babies were born, to cook and do laundry. I was so blessed to have her help each time. That morning she came in and placed a stack of freshly folded towels on the bed as she greeted me with a smile. I saw the same pride in her eyes I had seen so many years before, at such a simple thing as that stack of freshly laundered and perfectly folded towels.

I thought about how many times she had done that household chore in her lifetime; how it was simply commonplace for her—a complete afterthought. I recalled how, when I was a little girl, they magically appeared in the bathroom cabinet that way and how I went to bat several times in my life over the technique she taught me. I smiled back, even through the pain of my C-section healing, glad to know that we shared this one simple thing, always.

To this day I think of my mother when I fold towels. I will admit I have gone the way of half-and-half with the little kitchen towels, because they fit in the drawer better that way. However, there is no longer a dispute in our family about how to fold bath towels. My husband gave up his protestations long ago and likes the uniform way they look, all folded in the same manner. Although it's not often, every now and then when he does fold them, he does it the way I like. The children have been taught this technique as well. Someday they may also have to go to bat for what they believe is the correct method for folding towels. If so, I hope they will think of me and defend their learned towel-folding skills just as I have. After all, it is how their mom taught them—so it must be right.

Elaine Alguire is an uprooted Texan living in Cajun country with her three awesome kiddos and one husband. When not writing or photographing her kids or other people, she blogs at *The Miss Elaine-ous Life*, hangs on Twitter, and probably Facebook too. She is a Co-Producer for Listen To Your Mother in Southeast, Texas. Her writing has been featured on *Mamalode* and *BonBon Break* and an essay of hers was recently published in *Precipice, Volume III*.

Remember Not to Misplace Your Female Organs

By Patricia Walsh

Ruth Tierney was my beloved nana. She was my maternal guardian, my confidant, and my partner in crime. Nana was slight and always put together. That is to say her lipstick matched her slippers, which matched her nightgown. She saw no problem with wearing pajamas all day so long as they were coordinated. Nana was shy with new people. With my friends and me, she was just one of the girls. We relished teaching her the latest dance moves and telling her all the gossip.

When I was a child, Nana often sat on the side of my bed late into the night. She'd shake me and then ask, "Are you having trouble sleeping?" She would have tea and cookies already out on the kitchen table. I loved those late night indulgences. We had dozens of traditions that were "our special things," but tea and cookies was by far my favorite with her.

Nana hung on my every word, as I poured out my heart about the latest childhood tragedy. She was the master of empathy. I would go on about how the kids on the playground didn't want to play my game—the one with the convoluted plot about how we all had twins who had all been kidnapped by Ethiopians (because I didn't know what an Ethiopian was back then). Her response was always outrage on my behalf. I didn't understand until adulthood the gift of unconditional acceptance. Nana was in it with me, whatever it might be. When I cried, Nana cried too. We had a depth of connection that I long for as an adult.

My nana favored all things delicate and feminine. She often depicted me as her battered angel. There were many angel figurines around the house that were pristine and porcelain. There was also one of an angel with an ear-to-ear grin and scraped knees, depicted with the halo on upside down. I always had the sense that the angel with the scraped knees was me in Nana's eyes, because I was a rough and tumble kid. She would prefer I played with dolls.

One day she delighted, as I asked her to borrow some pots and pans to play house. She was ecstatic that I was showing interest in a feminine agenda. She was less excited when she found me in the pond near our house, using her fine pans to make mud pies to serve to frogs I'd captured in her Pyrex. She screamed when she discovered my jar of beetles in the refrigerator. When pressed to explain why I would do such a thing, I calmly explained that things in jars go in the fridge, just like the pickles and jam. I got in trouble for giving the pet turtle a bubble bath. I sat on the edge of my bed crying. I had never meant to hurt Frisbee. I had only meant to give him the royal treatment.

As I entered middle school, I dismissed the world of fashion and went full speed ahead toward a world of athletics. This continued into my high school years. My nana was socialized in the 1940s and 1950s. There was no Sporty Spice Girl in her generation. She had been brought up to believe women should be seen and not heard. She was fearful that my attention to *fitness* would make me less desirable to future husbands. I started receiving gifts of bright shiny pink dresses and vests, which didn't fit in with my 1990s flannel shirts and cargo pants. I came home from track practice one day in my high school team uniform. She covered her eyes and said, "I hope you didn't wear that in front of the boys!" Her voice was almost tearful.

As I grew up, we strained to understand each other. She wanted to understand what would make me try to be unattractive. I grew to be ever more athletic. Women of her generation were taught it was unattractive to be athletic. She feared for my future. *Would I marry? Would I have a fulfilled life?* I went on to win state metals and even went on to have Olympic potential in the triathlon. Every step of the way my nana had fear all over her face. Her pretty blue eyes cast gray. Her beautiful smile became a somber distant expressionless countenance.

I hated the divide between us. My partner in crime looked at me like I was a criminal. I had lots of friends, but nothing could fill that void. Our connection was unparalleled. As a seventeen-year-old junior in high school, I intuitively believed that what we needed to get back on track was one of our special things.

One day late at night I woke her up with tea and cookies. I needed to have one of those talks I remembered having as a child. I asked her about her concerns for my athletics.

I expected to hear her fear for my potential to find a partner. I expected to hear her concern regarding my attractiveness. What I did not expect was her fear for my physicality. She took my hand in hers, and in a concerned whisper explained to me that women who were too athletic could misplace their female organs; this leaves them unable to bare children. Her beautiful face, with the high cheekbones and deep-set eyes, had heartfelt terror all over it. She was imagining a nightmare in my future.

Even at the tender age of seventeen I knew this was an old wives' tale. I laughed out loud. I will forever regret laughing. Her forehead wrinkled, and she held her face in her palms. The fear on her face was now was replaced with hurt.

She had been speaking from the heart. She had been misinformed. She was repeating something she had been told; something that she believed. In that moment I drove the wedge in deeper. She put her heart on the table, and I showed her judgment.

She had demonstrated to me unconditional acceptance. No matter how childish or petty my fears or upsets had been, she was always on my side. No matter what, she felt my pain. My laugh, my dismissal of her trust, and my dismissal of her heart will forever haunt me. I'll never forget the hurt on her face. Our relationship had a blemish.

But thanks to my nana's unconditional love, we were eventually able to move on. I knew from then on, when a loved one is confiding, there is no value in judging their belief; there is only value in cultivating the connection and honoring the love between you. It would have been right to posture as a gentle educator. It was not right to dismiss her genuine concern.

As a long-time athlete, I'm reasonably assured that my female organs are still in place and seem to be staying there.

My nana's advice was sometimes off the mark. My nana's heart, sincerity, and hope for my future—they were always on point. Ruth Tierney passed in 2005. I have missed her every day and often wish I had someone to drink tea with in the late hours of the night. Today, I am a career athlete. I do hope beyond hope she would have grown to accept and embrace my dedication to my sport. She was right about one thing. She was absolutely right in saying potential suitors really don't like it when you are stronger than they are.

Diagnosed with a pediatric brain tumor, **Patricia Walsh** became blind at age five, due to surgery complications. Despite struggling with depression and hopelessness as a teenager, she is a world-champion triathlete and award-winning engineer. In 2009, she signed up for the Ironman and in 2011, she set the world record for blind athletes in the Ironman Distance, beating out previous records by over eighty minutes. Patricia holds a degree in Computer Science and Electrical Engineering and was one of the first blind engineers to work at Microsoft. Patricia is the three-time National Champion for the Paratriathlon and a two-time Bronze for the United States in Short Course World Championship. Patricia will represent the USA in the 2016 Paralympics in triathlon.

Was THAT on Sale?

By Ashley Alteman

I think the first word to drop out of my mouth as a baby was *SALE*. I'm fairly certain that my mother's frugal tendencies were programmed into my brain at the time of conception.

As a young child, I remember roaming through store clearance racks and popping out to scare the shit out of my mother and grandmother. My childlike behavior was quickly corrected, and I was trained and *overly* educated about the beauty of a sale. I knew what the yellow tags meant, the green tags, and for the love of all things holy, what the RED tags meant. Red tags were the heavy hitters. Red tags translated to: FIRE SALE; an already discounted item that was now reduced by an even larger percentage—AKA the jackpot of sales.

By grade school, I was well on the *clearance bandwagon* with my mother and would hunt for deals with her each weekend.

New school shoes? *We had that shit covered.*

Broken crock pot? *BAM! A 50 percent off coupon, plus an early bird doorbuster sale!*

My mother and I were *on.top.of.it.* We made the best mother-daughter doorbuster duo.

I was the only kid in the third grade who could tell you where to buy an entire Cornishware dish set for under forty dollars. I was raised to seek out deals. I'm similar to one of those gymnasts born from two gymnast parents who just *knew* their child would be born a backflipping Olympian. Except my father hates shopping, and I couldn't do a somersault to save my life. Who knows, maybe my father was actually some discount-hunting milkman.

I digress.

Over the years I stuck to my hardcore sale tactics. Later in life, I met a man who was equally as frugal as I was. He'd complete the *Monopoly* grocery store games with me after each grocery-shopping trip in hopes of winning the one-million-dollar prize, only to be rewarded with a free loaf of bread. It was a match made in Heaven, so obviously, I had to marry him. There were a *few* other things I liked about him, but the love of a good deal really won my heart.

As I aged, I was introduced to eBay, Amazon, Craigslist, and Nordstrom Rack. Anything and everything was considered fair game if I believed in my bones that it was a good deal and that my mother would agree.

I took my mother's advice and really upped the ante. Anything that had a tag that listed a lower price than the originating price, I was in—and I was in *BIG.*

Oh, you save a ton of money if you sign up for auto-renewal with this organic cleaning supply company? *Count me in!*

What? If I sign up for the Amazon credit card, I receive 30 percent off my first purchase? *CHECK!*

Amazon Prime equals free shipping *and* free video streaming? *DOUBLE CHECK!*

Needless to say, over the years my mother's lesson of the "great deal" sort of backfired on me. I mean, I can still scope out a great deal, however, my problem now is that I can scope out about three hundred deals each time my hooves step out my front door. Literally.

A few months back, my husband and I noticed that the neighbors across the street were holding an estate sale. We walked on over to take a peek.

Turns out, this little old lady had phenomenal taste and, even more so, the people holding the estate sale had absolutely no idea that a Dolce & Gabbana coat should sell for a wee bit more than eight dollars. I left with a sack of greatness that would put Santa's Christmas sleigh to shame.

Recently, I've been getting calls from family members asking why I never respond to their emails. Nine times out of ten, I have no idea what they are talking about. The reason being, I have myself signed up for so many online and department store email lists with the promise of discount codes and first peek at sales, that all other emails are pushed down the line within a matter of seconds. At any given moment, I have about four thousand three hundred twenty-seven emails in my inbox. I keep it that way—because you never *really* know when you might need a coupon to go skydiving or a coupon for a new wireless router.

My problem is that the Internet was introduced to the world during my formative years where my mother had nothing but the Sunday paper and word of mouth about sales. I got sucked into the vortex of online marketing and online shopping.

She surely trained me up the way to go. I just largely departed from it.

Time to check my email!

Ashley Alteman is known for her love of dinosaurs, ponies wearing sweaters, and overuse of commas. She is an editor's nightmare. She won a spelling bee in the eighth grade for correctly spelling *carrot* and knew from that moment she was destined to be an amazing journalist (or a sarcastic blogger). She went with the latter. You can find her at *SmashleyAshley.com,* where she details her laugh-out-loud parenting and personal fails, and as a regular contributor at *BLUNTmoms.*

The Ball-Busting Career Woman

By Michelle Grewe

Soaking the kitchen table in tears on my first few hours back home from getting kicked out of college, I don't think I could have possibly expressed the guilt in a manner worthy of expression. No matter how many times I recapped the story highlighting that, "It wasn't exactly my fault," my father refused to find any understanding or pity for me.

Normally, the kitchen table lectures were reserved for him. That kitchen table was his biggest pulpit followed by the car, but for once my mistake was so severe and costly he really had no words for me.

My mother was always the nurturer. If my father said *no*, my sister and I knew to ask Mom. She never said *no*. Instead she said, "We'll see," which meant "probably not." Love always hopes. But that's why she never really lectured me. She wasn't designed to criticize.

She calmed me down with her soothing, *I love you* voice. "Getting kicked out of college is no big deal." Just hearing those words gave me a chance to finally exhale and see the apocalyptic situation for what it was: a mistake. Then my mother continued, changing her voice into a voice of God, "HOWEVER! Getting pregnant while in college, now that's a BIG deal." It was her way of saying, "Things can always be worse," and, "Make sure you don't forget to take your birth control pill, and try not to be a trollop."

Before protesting such a lecture, let me first explain that my mother was (and is) a feminist in the truest sense. Regardless of what her conscious opinion might've been, she lived her life as such that her primary goal was to have a career, and becoming a mother was secondary. Though once she had kids, her kids were her primary mission with her job taking a back seat. Nowadays, I'm not sure she knows how to do anything for herself besides work.

My mother's retirement will come more as a shock to me than her death simply because I have never seen that woman without a job. After high school, she went to college where she majored in Music. It was one talent my grandmother encouraged in all her daughters. When my mother had my sister and me, she took a break from teaching to work part-time for my father's radio station. When my sister and I started going to school she slowly re-entered the workforce, gaining experience at the private school we attended followed by teaching some college classes. Then we moved, and she joined the county's school system. As a result of motherhood, she had to work from the bottom-up a second time.

A secondary income from a man wasn't something she could count on. She married her first husband, a wife abuser. The first time he hit her was on their wedding day, and she continued with the marriage because of all the hard-earned dollars my grandparents forked out for the wedding. For a couple years, this man beat my mother profusely while she desperately made sure she was on birth control in fear of bringing a child into that environment. At some point, enough was enough, so she left him. Her second husband was my father, and when my father passed away from cancer, she remarried a third (with moments of separation during their current marriage).

The moral of the story is words my mother has said to me more than once. Quoteworthy words I will never forget.

"Men come and go, but a college degree will stay with you your entire life."

She faced abuse, cancer and grief, and family dysfunction, and through all those moments, her college degree and career kept her independent enough to get through the tough times. My sister and I have never wanted for anything, and it's only because of my mother's hard work and determination that she was able to always provide for us.

Despite her fiercely independent nature, the hardest part of motherhood for my mother was my sister and me leaving home. Your birthday becomes your child's birthday. Whatever life you led before motherhood is long forgotten. You embrace chaos for decades making every aspect of your life about your children, and then suddenly, you end up with an empty nest of peace, loneliness, and boredom.

Even after fleeing the coop, she reminded me, "People come and go. College degrees are life-long."

Unfortunately, I didn't follow her wonderful advice. My college experience was a series of one-night stands—not one-night stands of sex, but a bunch of college majors—strung together like Christmas lights with no plug. I love learning, but I don't appreciate being forced to pay large quantities of money for a piece of paper that makes me just as qualified for the same jobs as I qualified prior.

But I do agree with my mother that a woman should have a career. I have seen some women quit a career prospect to spend a lifetime of slaving after their families in the name of love, and they are miserable. As motherhood kicked me out of the workforce and dragged me home, I have found myself neglecting housewife duties to write or design something. I can't be in a place that doesn't utilize my creative strengths. While contributing to the overall household finances is important to me, it's not even really about the money. My need for a career is a self-actualizing one.

I remind you, my mother comes from an era where it wasn't common for a female to obtain a college degree. She was one of the first women who paved the way for equal opportunity. No matter what her relationship threw at her, she was always able to remain independent because she had that college degree.

My mom received a master's degree in Counseling and is one of the most certified people in our state in Counseling and Education. Those degrees not only helped her find better paying jobs within the school system, but also provided opportunities for part-time teaching jobs with universities and part-time counseling jobs in the summer. Meanwhile, her talent in singing and playing multiple instruments, including the piano, has kept her employed part-time as a church Music Director.

Because my mother fearlessly entered that world, she raised me to do the same; she raised me to use my mind as a primary tool while regarding the dishes and laundry as secondary things we did in the off-hours of the day. She is the reason I felt like I belonged in the military, enough to enlist. She is the reason nothing could bring me down no matter how hard or difficult my time was. My NCO once told me the reason he hated me so much was because, "You came in here with your big shot, East Coast attitude and took over." Hell yeah I did. My mother raised a leader.

I think some modern-day feminists sometimes confuse what feminism is really about. It's not about a woman complaining that the world is unequal. It's about women, like my mother, who simply didn't give a shit if it was equal or not. She just marked her territory and moved forward. She has dealt with every kind of asshole the world has had to offer yet still emerged with her womanly ways. She was submissive when it helped her and put her foot down when it was necessary.

Women like my mother are role models. Women like my mother are exactly what it means to be a woman.

Michelle Grewe is a mom, veteran, monster hitman, bouncer, twenty questions master, semi-professional diamond thief, mad scientist, human jungle gym, and a terrible driver. She paints, blogs at *Crumpets and Bollocks*, plays piano badly, and dabbles in T-shirt design and font-o-graphy. She also doesn't fold underwear and eats loads of gluten.

Hold the Phone, Except When at the Table

By Tiffany Marshall

Some kids had parents whose version of teaching manners was to remind them to say "please" and "thank you," as they headed out the door to a friend's house. My mom had a different strategy.

It wasn't enough that we were the only kids in Albuquerque, New Mexico, required by our Southern parents to say "ma'am" or "sir" instead of "what?" or "huh?" when we were called. There were strict guidelines about how we were to answer the telephone too.

In those days, the telephone was attached to the wall by a cord. The base of the phone was connected to the handset by another cord—a curly, stretchy one that was always tangling itself. All four members of our family shared one phone number, and if someone happened to be on the phone when someone else tried to call, they'd get a busy signal. It was just one step above having the operator connect us.

So, if the phone rang, and I thought it might be for me, or if my parents were unable to get to the phone before the caller gave up and hung up (answering machines didn't exist yet), I would answer. "Marshall residence. Tiffany speaking." Those were the rules. It's like I worked for them (which I did, in a way) and our home was a place of business (which it wasn't). Adults who called were impressed by my professionalism: people from my dad's office, other parents, telemarketers. My friends teased me at first, until they got used to the process of calling my house.

The worst was when the parent of a friend told their child, who happened to be in my class at school, how I'd answered the phone and that child mocked me by repeating the phrase to my entire fourth grade class. But those were the rules. If I answered the phone, that's how I had to answer regardless of any torment I got from my peers.

Other lessons Mom taught me about using the phone included:

- Appropriately identifying myself before asking to speak with a friend: "Hello. This is Tiffany. May I please speak to Laura?"

- Using proper grammar: "This is she" not "This is her" in response to a caller who asked for me when I was the one who answered.

- Addressing a wrong number: "I'm sorry. There's nobody here by that name."

- When my parents weren't home, or were on the toilet, and I didn't know the caller: "I'm sorry. They can't come to the phone right now. May I take a message?"

The phone rules were non-negotiable, and I honored them as I grew older and wanted to use the phone more and more often.

Mom also taught us table manners. They went something like this:

- Wash your face and hands before coming to the table. Use soap. Don't just wipe your dirty hands on the towel. Sniff and sight tests are always a possibility.

- Place your napkin in your lap before taking the first bite of food. Children who forget this step must leave the table, go to their bedroom, and count to ten out loud before returning to the table and trying again—much to the amusement of the other sibling.

- Never say, "I don't like that," or you'll receive an additional helping and sit at the table until you've eaten it all.

- No burping, farting, or discussion of the two at the table. (That rule was amended as my little brother got older and gassier. The rule shifted to saying, "Excuse me," after the fact.)

- Ask for something to be passed, instead of reaching across the table for it. Violators caught in the act might get poked by a fork.

- Ask to be excused before getting up from the table. Asking does not guarantee permission to leave the dinner table.

• Take your dishes to the sink. Failure to do so will result in returning from whatever fun activity you're currently engaged in to clear the entire table.

Not all rules had to be enforced with corporal punishment or verbal praise. Sometimes it was just easier to keep the rule than it was to break it. Seatbelts fell into that category.

Mom drove a classic, two-door Monte Carlo for most of my growing up years. It only had lap belts for safety restraints. No matter. Mom had been in a terrible car accident before she married my dad and credited the seatbelt with saving her life. As her children, we would not be in a moving vehicle without a seatbelt on. In fact, she wanted to hear the *click* before the car was put into gear, regardless of how late we were or how urgently we told her we'd fasten it as she drove.

To this day, she still tells my brother to put his seatbelt on. (I'm in the habit at this point in my life.) He's under the impression that a freshly ironed shirt remaining wrinkle free is more important than wearing a seatbelt that would cause wrinkles. You can't blame Mom for trying, but he comes by his stubbornness naturally.

Mom raised us to be independent, saying things like, "I'm not going to be your judge and jury. The two of you need to settle it," or, "I'm not your referee," when we'd come to her to solve a dispute between the two of us or among the neighbor kids. Part of that independence training included learning to clean up after ourselves.

Our bedrooms were our responsibility and our place of privacy. If Mom looked into our closets and deemed them unfit, she motivated us to clean them by saying, "Clean your closet, or I will." Perhaps the millennial generation would take her up on the offer, but my brother and I didn't want her to get rid of stuff we wanted to keep, put things where we couldn't find them, or find things we considered *secret* (like the notes we passed in class (the predecessor of text messages), or diaries (the predecessor of social media), or our bubblegum stash).

The threat worked because she'd been known to follow through on it if we failed to meet her demands in a timely manner.

Of all her lessons, it was the creative ones that really stuck. I learned early on to hold the phone, except when at the table.

Tiffany Marshall: Blogger. Technical jargon translator. Online marketer. Small business advocate. Youth worker. Waterskier. Mentor. Reader. College football enthusiast. *Big Bang Theory* fan. Brainstormer. Entrepreneur. Humorist. Not necessarily in that order. Follow Tiffany on her blog, *The Everyday Gospel*.

Hypothetical Needles

By Jennifer Wirth

In San Francisco, there's a beach near the Sunset where all busses end. At night it becomes a strange gathering place, where the homeless intersect with drunken middle-class teenagers. I once found myself there, being my mother. I was neither drunk nor homeless, but I had wandered onto Ocean Beach with the romantic idea of seeing the full moon suspended above the moody Pacific.

As I approached the beach, I felt the sensation of taking flight. There was a raw energy to the place as ragged men with shopping carts gathered for chitchat in front of the dunes. The street was alive—cars zoomed past me, fearlessly weaving through traffic. It was nearly midnight, and I couldn't help but wonder why these people weren't in bed yet.

I stood at a crosswalk in front of the beach and noticed it was covered in a layer of persistent sand. I was with my boyfriend and two of our friends. When we got together, it felt like we could see magic. We delighted in the abnormal and didn't think twice about swimming around in our imaginations. But now, as we plunged forward on the sandy surface of the beach, I felt detached from their psychedelic, mystical conversation. My mind had shifted from youthful observation to an unwavering fear. At any moment, I could step on a needle.

The situation kidnapped me from the present. My friend's voices drifted into the distance, and my eyes fixated on my feet. I was wearing sandals, and each time I took a step, the top of my foot dipped down into the sand. My heart picked up speed, and I stiffened my limbs. I tried desperately to walk on top of the sand instead of in it, but it was no use. My sandals were full of sand, and the group plowed forward in the comfort of their closed-toed shoes. I didn't have to wrack my brain to identify the source of my fear; needles had been a popular topic of discussion throughout my childhood.

A few weeks after this incident, I shared the beach story with my mother as we prepared Thanksgiving dinner.

"You made me, like, obsessively afraid of drug needles," I'd proclaimed over a pile of chopped carrots.

My mother hung her head and laughed, "Okay, but come on! People are, you know," she paused, searching for the right word, "freaky!"

My boyfriend and I laughed with her, and later he told me that watching my mother and me together was like seeing me in a mirror. This was something I was used to hearing, but for the first time in my life I began to see it too. I would catch myself talking like her and using the same hand gestures while speaking. Even the ways we arranged our sentences and told stories were comparable.

I grew up in a middle-class family in a small agriculture town near Sacramento. In my youth I hated it, but the older I get, the more I cherish the idea of growing up with open fields and the smell of the tomato cannery running in the summertime. There was a field of sunflowers next to my high school that seemed to stretch for miles; every morning the flowers would face east, and as I drove home from school they would face west. Things moved like clockwork. Life wasn't perfect, but it was familiar and it wasn't scary.

Regardless, I was growing up on the brink of PC culture, and there were a lot of rules. At my house, one of those rules was "Never touch a needle." I remember my mother gripping my arm with a protective tightness near the playground. She was crouched down, eye-to-eye with me, desperately trying to get my distracted gaze to focus on her.

"If you see a needle in the sand, do not touch it. Don't even to show me. Just leave it, and don't touch it." In my memory, she was beautiful when she was speaking to me. Her eyes were big, colored like almonds, and the sun was bringing out tones of red in her brown hair.

I don't blame my mother for having the fears that she did. Now, when I see my nieces and nephew playing, fully immersed in an innocent world of fairies and pirates, I so desperately want them to be shielded from bad things. On Christmas, my oldest niece pulled her aunt aside and asked, "Is Santa really coming, or is it just a big joke?"

Her face wrinkled with genuine concern, and I began to realize that the process of growing up could be incredibly painful. I think my mother saw how much joy I had in my life and didn't want anyone to steal it away from me. She wanted me to be safe and happy, but she also didn't want me to be naïve.

When I was in second grade, I went out trick-or-treating with my best friend and her sister. We scoured the neighborhood like little monsters, knocking and walking until our feet were sore. At home, I snuggled up with my mom in her bed, and we dumped out my bag of candy. I told her about a weird, old lady that wanted to give us unwrapped chocolates from one of those See's candy boxes, and how I'd proudly said, "No, thank you," as if I were turning down a cigarette. This process of checking the candy felt commonplace to me, and when I saw my friends eating candy without their moms checking it, I thought it was a little strange. I'd asked my friend, "Doesn't your mom have to look at your candy before you eat it?" She'd nodded her head, "No," and smiled with a mouth full of Skittles.

My mom explained that she had to check the candy to make sure it hadn't been opened and that no small holes had been poked in it. She said that people could take needles and inject things like drugs into it. The possibilities for needles seemed to be endless: they could be lurking in a sandbox, at the bottom of a McDonalds' ball pit, and even tucked between the cushions in a taxicab.

I can remember my parents getting in a small argument over that last one. We were visiting San Francisco for the weekend. It was my first trip there with my little brother. We stayed in a hotel near the Warf and Financial District, and the bathroom had a TV. I remember sitting next to my mother, watching a black-and-white movie while she took a bath, my eyes darting between the small screen and our reflection in the mirror.

We saw a lot of tourist sights on our trip, and my dad was dying to take a cab down Lombard Street. My mom didn't want to, and I couldn't understand why. Finally, I remember her hissing sideways at my dad, "You don't get it Jim. They're dirty. There could be needles in the cushions, and I don't want the kids touching one." My dad had looked at my mother with an expression that said, "You're crazy," and she watched nervously as he hailed a cab. She turned to my brother and me, with her familiar stern expression, and warned us not to stick our fingers in the cushions, to sit still, and to look at the seats before we plopped ourselves down.

I still follow her cab rules. I can see her as my hands move while I tell a story, and I hear her voice, masked as my voice, as I walk across a sandy beach at night. It makes me feel comforted to know that she's out there and that she loves me. In the moments when I feel her fears, and realize that they've become my own, I can also feel the impermanence of being alive. The falsity of being me becomes clearer, and it helps me see less of a difference between me, my friends, the homeless men at the beach, and the hypothetical needles forgotten in the sand.

Jennifer Wirth is a writer and poet living in Northern California. She holds a B.A. in Creative Writing from Sonoma State University, where she served as Senior Editor to the literary magazine *ZAUM* Vol. 16. Her work has appeared in *Foodie Daily* and *Biz Marketing* magazines.

Nothing Attractive About a Drunk Girl

By Julia Arnold

"Just remember," my mom often warned us in a lilting voice, "there's nothing attractive about a drunk girl."

While most involved parents probably warn their kids about the frightening health-related risks of drinking too much—say, *alcohol poisoning*—or remind them that one can get taken advantage of with too much alcohol flowing through the body, my mother's seemingly lighthearted last words to my sister and me before we headed out for a night on the town were of a different ilk.

My sister is four years older than I am, but as luck would have it, she enrolled in graduate school at the university where I was an undergraduate. Together, we were ready to take the world by storm, and after gleefully obtaining every college kid's Holy Grail (a fantastic fake ID), I was able to accompany her at the wee age of nineteen to all of the college bars to do just that.

My sister and I may have been proud feminists, seriously studying modern poetry (me) and law (her) for hours most days of the week, but on a Friday or Saturday night (and perhaps the odd Thursday or Tuesday), we let loose. Even over the phone, my mom must have sniffed out our top weekend priority: to have fun. *Lots* of it.

Surprisingly, her seemingly simple warning often worked to keep us breathing and somewhat humiliation-free on some nights more than others.

Nothing could make us laugh harder than when we contemplated ordering that third drink, while the other one slowly nodded her head, recalling the quote, "There's nothing attractive about a drunk girl." Laughter was probably not what my mom intended, but how could we not find it hilarious, yet completely pertinent at a bar surrounded by (and sometimes being) the very people she warned us not to be?

When pressed, we had our defensive pleas, "Come on, Mom, everyone drinks in college. It's no big deal. And what exactly do you mean anyway?"

My mom was pleased to elaborate in excruciating detail, "If you've seen it once, you've seen it a thousand times. The running mascara; the slurring speech; the cigarette hanging out of the mouth; the drunken crying and fighting. None of it is attractive. If I know anything, I know you don't want to be like *that*." She painted a clear enough picture. Virtuous or not, my sister and I certainly didn't want to fall into the sloppy, unattractive category that our mother described so well.

While her words may not have stopped us every time from ordering that ill-advised syrupy margarita, they definitely helped. Because one thing was for sure, we didn't want to ruin a night—and waste a great outfit—by drunkenly crying about nothing in the crowded bathroom, black tears running down our cheeks, all because we chugged too much cheap beer from the watered-down keg.

She likely saved us a lot of grief in our partying days. In fact, looking back now, I can fairly attribute many hangover-less days of my youth to my mom's one simple admonishment, not to mention our ability to (usually) avoid the embarrassing perils of drunkenly staggering home with guys eager to show us more than just their poster-clad dorm rooms.

For all of this, I owe my mother an infinite round of thanks. My sister and I both managed to come out of our late teens and twenties alive, and we currently appear sane and stable to the naked eye.

While the free-spirited Saturday nights of our collegiate days are over, my mother's infamous warning has taken on a new relevance in my current life as a mother to two young children. It now translates to something along the lines of, "There's nothing attractive about a hungover mom."

Again, her words are surprisingly relevant and, more importantly, *effective*. When home with tiny, needy offspring, there is nothing worse than having to divvy up frozen waffles and sippy cups of milk at 6:30 a.m., especially when you feel like complete and total crap. The misery is far worse when you have brought it upon yourself by drinking too much celebrating the previous evening's long overdue date night. Remembering her words often helps me linger over just one or two glasses of wine, rather than regretfully downing an entire bottle.

I wonder if I will remember to repeat my mom's wise words of warning when my own dear daughter, the squishy-cheeked, independent one so fond of insisting, "I do it myself," is of partying age. Will I solemnly discuss the many dangers of drinking in hopes of scaring her from making embarrassing, drunken mistakes, or will I draw upon my mother's clever approach?

What I do know for sure is this: well-played, Mom. Well. Freaking. Played.

Julia Arnold is a freelance writer living in the Twin Cities with her husband and two small children. She writes about the less glamorous side of motherhood on her popular blog, *Frantic Mama*. Her work has been featured in numerous publications including the humor anthology *Clash of the Couples*, as well as in *Mamalode*, Felicity Huffman's *What The Flicka?*, *Scary Mommy*, and more.

Behind Every Ugly Sun

By Shannon Day

The art of patience. You've got it mastered, Mom. You disagree when I say this, and I know you're not a total expert, but you really are good. I should know, right? Over the years, our mother-daughter dynamic has offered many a platform, from which you've shown commendable strength. And now that I'm a mom, those heated moments are revisited. I know the spotlight shines brightly on me.

My daughters are watching. They're taking it all in. Maybe someday they'll even write stories about me. I'm sure to, at the very least, inspire a few Facebook updates in the years to come.

So the pressure is on.

I know I'll never master the art of patience, but I try. I try to stay calm when I feel the warning rumbles of the volcano within. I reach further for that last bit of strength when I'm dangling on the edge of motherhood's cliff, with nothing but a partnerless sock to cling to.

But sometimes, my efforts aren't enough. The volcano erupts. I lose my grip and into a rage I slip. I snap and shout like a crazy woman, and I disappoint myself and my kids. After the snap, my motherly guilt sets in, and I rock in my theoretical corner until I can process it. I don't stay there for long, though.

When I'm ready, I let it go. I take a few deep breaths, and I vow to try harder and to do better next time. This is what you've taught me, Mom. To be patient. Patient with, and kind to, myself.

I apologized years ago for forcing you to master the art of patience during my hormone-infused teen years. It wasn't until I moved away from home that I started to realize just how selfish I'd been, and just how amazing you are.

I was starting to see.

All the little bubbles that I'd been living in were beginning to burst. I was discovering just how small each of us really are. I was tiny. Yet to you, I was the most important person in the world. It was starting to sink in; I was suddenly desperate to share with you my *realizations*.

So I wrote a very deep and meaningful letter of thanks and appreciation. I also painted a picture of a sun for you. It was a colorful, amateur-looking spectacle that signified new beginnings. I was going through an ugly painting phase at that time. (Yes, I was twenty-one and not ten. Sorry about that.) But despite my lack of artistic flare, you were grateful for the recognition and the apology. You hung the painting up in the spare bedroom; although, come to think of it, I haven't seen it lately.

But that's okay. The point is, we were able to move on to the next phase of our relationship. You see, when I left home, I gained some insight into just how lucky I really am.

In my first year of university life, I met a friend whose mother had passed away when she was two. This friend had spent her life wondering what her mom had been like, while mourning the loss of the relationship they never got to have. You were always there for me, yet I had taken you for granted.

I later met a friend whose mother was jealous of her. She intentionally made her daughter's life more difficult by sabotaging her happiness. You always supported me and lifted me up. I hadn't appreciated what a gift that was.

I also met a friend who was very close to her mom. They were like two pees in a happy pod. I had never been open to that kind of relationship with you. You were willing, but I was stubborn and too wrapped up in my own life to consider it.

You knew I'd come around, though. Didn't you? I was overtly (fingers in my ears) not listening to you back then. But you sent your messages home anyway, and I learned from you. You led your life knowing that I was watching. You weren't perfect. You never claimed to be. But you were supportive, patient, and loving.

I am blessed to have three wonderful daughters. I'll do my best to be those things for them. I sure would love to earn their version of an ugly sun painting someday, or at least make it to the other side of the teen years with our relationship intact. So I'd better get versed in the art of patience, right? Especially now, with my eldest settling nicely into tweenhood.

My little tween is very much a miniature version of me. And with one feisty foot stomp, I'm transported back to the days when I was in her shoes (she has Converse, just like I did), and you were in mine (thankfully our footwear is not the same; it was the 1980s after all). And, during those heated moments, I *will* my patience to be more like yours. Often it is. But sometimes I'm caught unprepared, like first thing in the morning before I've had coffee or at the end of the day when I'm running on empty.

And just like that, I slip—

That's why I'll continue to aim for master status even though I'll never be an expert. I'll hone my skills, and I won't crash or smash or break when I slip off of motherhood's cliff, partnerless sock in hand. Hell no! Instead, I'll bounce. (Not like a trampoline bounce, because we moms know how that can go.) Just a gentle bounce to get me back on my feet, because behind every ugly sun is a new beginning. And new beginnings are what family is all about. *Right, Mom?*

Shannon Day is wife to one gorgeous, yet slightly overbearing *Brit* and mom to three little ladies. Once a teacher, now a story-maker and occasional cocktail shaker, she shares her tales, martini recipes, and her shenanigans at *Martinis & Motherhood*. Shannon is a regular contributor to *BLUNTmoms* and is co-founder of Tipsy Squirrel Press. Find her on *Scary Mommy, Mamalode, Mamapedia*, and *In the Powder Room*.

A Half-Full Glass of Happiness

By Janine Huldie

Staring at a blank screen with a flashing cursor—

I know I want to write and convey here how recently my life has been anything but straight forward or simple. Don't get me wrong, I hate sounding like I'm whining, or complaining, or even venting, but I guess this will be a bit of all three. It isn't my usually style to be honest. I'm usually pretty damn good at sucking it up and just moving forward.

This wasn't always the case. As a teen, I used to constantly find the negative in most things, and talked about it whenever I could.

Actually, I remember my mom telling me, "Can't you just see the glass half full not empty for once?" (I was probably about sixteen—a young girl and hormonal, need I say more?)

I'm not even sure what I had been complaining about— probably a boy, because back then the biggest problems were usually over the opposite sex. My teen years were filled with boy-caused angst and drama on any given day.

My mother's advice didn't necessarily define me, but I do remember thinking back then that I should try my best to indeed see life with a more positive attitude. Not exactly with rose-colored glasses, but at the very least I didn't need to be a Debbie Downer or someone just waiting to explode when the next problem arose.

I was able to somewhat apply her advice in my late teens. Now, for the most part, I see life with a rosier perspective. Sometimes, I even repeat to myself that things could always be worse and that the glass is definitely more than half full! *Trust me, I know I am lucky and life is relatively good.* I was fortunate to have grown up in a fairly normal, loving family. Did I have moments where I thought the people around me were crazy? Hell yes, but still they stuck with me through thick and thin—loving me even when I thought I was unlovable.

Then I married a man who is my equal—honest, loving, my best friend, and a wonderful father. Do we have our moments and fights? Again, hell to the yes, but still I wouldn't want to fight or make up with anyone else.

The cherry on top are my two girls—yes, I grew up to be a girly girl, so getting two of my own was a blessing in disguise. They are perfect in my eyes, despite having their own moments when they're anything but faultless. But they are still mine, and to that end, they will always be perfect.

Recently, my older daughter, Emma, had been pretty sick. Like I said, I try my best to see the positive in things, but dealing with healthcare and doctors and not feeling like the appropriate care was being given—twice to her own pediatrician and once to urgent care after hours before she finally got diagnosed as having pneumonia—was nothing short of infuriating.

I somehow made it through the experience with my sanity (barely) intact. I even managed not to punt the girl's pediatrician after he callously informed me, "You do know we're on call night and day even if the office is closed, right? You could have called and left a message on Friday for us to get back to you instead of taking her to urgent care."

Gritting through my teeth, I answered calmly and succinctly, "I'm this child's mother ... remember I carried her for nine-plus months and then safely delivered her into this world. I'm not going to even begin to defend my actions to you and maybe you should take that finger you are pointing at me and turn around to the other doctor in your practice who sent us away a week ago at the onset of Emma being sick to buy over-the-counter nasal drops at CVS, because as she told us, 'Her chest is clear.' Let's concentrate on *that* instead of pointing fingers ... okay?"

Finally, after all the turmoil, we had a diagnosis and prescription medication; it only took a week and my tenacious persistence.

That is until–

Emma was finally feeling well enough to go back to school. I made sure to get her folder ready the night before, with all her make-up work, plus include her note for lunch and even put her snack bag together. But when I went to get her ready in the morning, I realized it was library day. And like clockwork, her book was missing.

"Emma, where is your library book?"

God love her, she looked, but told pretty evenly, "I don't know where it is, Mommy."

Panic took the wheel. After asking again calmly, and then not so calmly (yes, some words I'm not so proud of came exhausting out of me), it was found on our kitchen table under my husband's laptop.

I then rushed to get the antibiotic into her before leaving for school. The medicine was liquid and needed to be shaken first. I loosened the cap and set it down while searching for the medicine cup. And doing a million other things at the same time. When I grabbed for the bottle again, I immediately shook it, spewing a white chalky mess all over everything. I stood there for about ten seconds, before my eyes welled with tears. I couldn't even manage to put myself back together right away.

In between sobbing my eyes out, my hysteria funneled toward my husband, "Shit! You need to call the doctor to get more medicine!"

"I have to get to work. I'm late already. You'll have to call," he calmly informed me.

"No way, I'm already a mess, and if I call, they're going to cart me off to the nut house! Seriously, there is no chance in hell I'm calling the doctor. I just can't." It was a totally less-than-perfect, glass half-empty moment from me and yet—

Not only did my husband clean up the spilled medicine, but he also called to get more and even got Emma's first of two dosages for the day into her, all while letting me have a meltdown, as well as put myself (Humpty Dumpty style) back together piece-by-piece.

Even after my less than stellar performance as a mom that morning, as well as acting like a wife straight out of a horror movie, everyone forgave me.

Moral of this tale:

I guess sometimes I have to concede that I can't do it all—I definitely can't please all people all of the time. I have to just accept that I'm not perfect, and I make my fair share of mistakes and messes.

And still, my glass, as my mother taught me long ago, is most definitely half full, not empty, by any means.

Janine Huldie was previously a licensed middle school teacher who became a stay-at-home mom after having her second daughter. She was born and raised in NYC, but now resides with her family in the suburbs. She is a WAHM blogger at *Confessions of a Mommyaholic* and runs her own graphic design company at J9 Designs. She has two beautiful, zany, energetic daughters and a husband and is still trying (key word) to keep it all in perspective by attempting to make the days and nights a little bit brighter.

Things to Be Encountered Along the Road

By Briana Gervat

"Is she dead, Ma?" It was the only question that could be asked from the backseat by a three-year-old, after watching the front end of our family station wagon—driven by my mother—collide with a woman on a bike. She was not dead. She did not die. She simply got up, brushed herself off, and continued along her way as if nothing happened. She was lucky and so were we. This perfectly timed universe allowed us, and her, to keep going. As a child, this was one of my first lessons to be learned: these minor accidents, these bumps, sometimes big and sometimes small, were things to be encountered along the road.

These are the memories of my childhood; almost all of them begin in the car. In this car, we drove everywhere—west to Brooklyn and Manhattan and east to Montauk and East Marion. In the winter we drove north to the mountains of

Vermont and Canada. In the summer we always drove to the beach as if it was the only place in the world. On the way there our car was filled with hopes of adventures to be had and sand castles to be built. On the way home it was quiet, full of copper-toned babies, sun-tanned and sun-drunk, waiting for fireflies to light up the night.

From the back seat, I would watch my mother, curious as to what she thought about as she twirled her hair between her fingertips and watched as the world unfolded in front of her. By the time my mother had us, her own mother had not driven for years because she was fearful of the road. Sometimes I wondered how it had come to be that her daughter was so fearless, so confident behind the wheel. Sometimes my mother sang along with whatever song was playing on the radio. Sometimes she pointed out the window to the stars and the moon, to the thunder and the lightning, to everything that moved and to everything that stood still. And sometimes, like all good mothers, she threatened to pull the car over and leave us on the side of the road. Of course that never happened, but we were still young enough to believe that it could.

On these trips, both long and short, it was never just my parents and my brothers who came along for the ride. Our station wagon fit ten people, and I do not remember it ever being empty. It was always full; full of our extended family comprised of those related by blood and those that were not. It was a car full of memories; some that you wish could stay with you forever and some that you wish could be forgotten or erased, the ones you wished never happened at all.

After she was diagnosed with cancer, we would drive my aunt to chemotherapy. My mother at the wheel, my Aunt Linda by her side and the rest of us kids piled into the back. Years later, we drove to my aunt's funeral, and sometime after that, we drove to pick up my cousins, to bring them home to our house because they had nowhere else to live. My mother was once again behind the wheel, perhaps afraid to let go of the one thing in the world that she still had control over. It was then that I learned that not all rides are joyful; not all rides take you to the places you want to go.

The years passed and we traded our retro, wood-paneled station wagon for a sleek, straight-out-of-the-nineties Astrovan with doors that slid open from the side. It would never be as cool as our Ford Country Squire, but my mother drove it like it was going out of style.

As a teenager I don't remember how many times I slammed the car door and walked away promising never to return, angrier at the world than I was with her. When I finally sulked back to the car, she unlocked the door and let me back in without saying a word. In these moments the silence was palpable. It was a silence filled with disappointment, doubts, and misgivings. It was a silence filled with the infinite sorrow experienced between a teenage daughter, who believed she knew everything there was to know about the world, and her middle-aged mother, who had acquiesced to the unknown long before I was even born. On the way home, all that was heard was the rolling of tires along a road that never seemed to point our tumultuous relationship in the right direction.

And yet, despite the rocky roads of my teenage years, when I first got behind the wheel of a car, it was my mother who taught me how to drive. Whether she feared or rejoiced in my newfound freedom had yet to be determined. Now with her on the right side of the car and me on the left I could not help but notice her foot reaching for a brake pedal that was not there. I do not blame her for her lack of confidence in my driving abilities. I drove a little too fast, without enough caution and with reckless abandon. After all, I drove like her.

In the years before I received my license, full of the impatience of a youth in too much of a hurry to grow up, she only had to remind me of this: "You are only young for a certain amount of time and then it's gone."

When I finally was able to drive and had yet to learn the rules of the road, my mother always had gems, like my turns behind the wheel, which came in fits and starts. "If a car is passing you in the right lane, you are driving too slowly. The gas pedal can also be used as a break." But that was the thing about my mother. She never used her breaks when it came to me. My mother loves me at full speed.

There was an afternoon driving along the Long Island Expressway when the song "Ain't No Mountain High Enough" came on the radio. Snow was falling from the sky above, covering the ground and the road before us. In silent agreement we decided that she would be Tammy Terrell and I would be Marvin Gaye, and we sang with all of our might. The traffic grew still, and yet here we were more alive than the world outside of the four doors. It was as if life let us slow down for that moment, so that we might remember that I was her daughter and she was my mother, and there was nothing in this big old world that would keep either of us from getting to one another—not one thing.

When I needed to learn how to drive a stick, it was my mother who brought me to the parking lot at Sunken Meadow State Park and taught me that not everything in life comes automatically. She laughed and shook her head at the thought of me driving a rusty green 1989 Ford F-150 nine years my junior, but so much worse for the wear. She showed me how important it was to be gentle with the clutch for not all transitions are smooth; sometimes we stall, sometimes we hesitate, sometimes we forget what gear we are in. These shifts are what enable us to go fast or slow, forward or back, but always in perpetual motion, because the road rarely allows us to stand still.

In this life we do not always get a choice of what kind of road we are on, and we most certainly never get to choose who our mothers are, but if we are lucky, these mothers choose to stick by our side, alternating between driver and passenger, applying the brakes when necessary but always, always, always encouraging us to drive.

A native New Yorker, **Briana Gervat** graduated from the University of Mary Washington in 2002 with a B.A. in Art History, where she also played lacrosse for the Eagles. Equal parts poet, art critic, and writer of memories, Briana recently received her M.A. in Art History from the Savannah College of Art and Design with a focus on art that rises from the ashes of war. After graduating from SCAD, she travelled to Rwanda for two months to continue her research on the Rwandan Genocide and the art and artists of East Africa. She now lives in New York City, where she is writing about life in Rwanda, twenty years later.

Hat Trick

By Hope Sunderland

"She's really, really sick," my father said, his voice trembling. He'd called to tell me my mother was in the hospital. "You'd better come now."

Several months had passed since my last trip home. My busy life hadn't yielded a natural break for a visit, but I couldn't risk putting it off any longer. I rearranged work and car pool assignments, stocked the pantry, wrote extensive lists for my family, and taped the notes to the refrigerator door.

I packed the car for the long drive and set out early the next morning. A few blocks from home, I remembered a gift I had already purchased for my mother for Christmas, which was still several months away. She might not make it until then. So I turned the car around, pulled back into the garage, and ran into the house to grab the present from a high shelf in the hall closet. I stashed it on the shotgun seat beside me.

When I arrived, I immediately went to the hospital. Mom looked small and pale, almost blending in against the white of the hospital sheets. Her breathing was labored with oxygen hissing through plastic pronged tubing in her nose. When she talked, she erupted into coughing fits and stopped often to catch her breath.

After a hug and some small talk, I set the box I'd brought on the bed beside her. "I couldn't resist this," I said, faking more enthusiasm than I felt. "This darling, little red number is you."

She glanced at the box, but made no effort to open it. So I untied the bow and plucked a hat out of the paisley-patterned round box and settled it on my head. The small hat was red, my mother's favorite color, adorned with a perky red feather and matching veil. It begged to be perched at a jaunty angle. I tried it on and did a few twirls and Vogue poses. Mom smiled weakly. The sudden thought that she might never get to wear it made my throat tighten. I pulled the veil down to hide my tears.

My mother had a long history with hats, something we somewhat shared. My infant snapshots usually had me wearing a ruffled baby bonnet, tied under my chin with satin ribbons. During pre-school hot summers, I played on our shaded front porch and made sun hats out of flat white paper plates, decorating them with crayons and using yarn scraps for ties. I clomped around the porch modeling them in Mom's old high heels.

I always got a new hat for Easter, sometimes homemade to match a hand-stitched dress. On Easter Sunday, we'd pile into our family station wagon and sing a rousing rendition of "In Your Easter Bonnet" on the way to church.

My mother and I fancied hats in any style: large brimmed or small, feathers, veils, ribbons, plain or ornamental, saucy, and sassy. We liked the jaunty air they stirred in us. My mother taught me that hats had special powers to lift a woman's spirit.

Hats needed attitude. My mother had panache, and she knew it. She was raised in an era when a real lady wouldn't be caught dead at a church service or PTA meeting without a hat. Hats were a competition to her. She was proud of her reputation at church for her stunning hats. Other ladies sometimes sought to outdo her style; the men sought not to sit in the pew behind her. If hats were an Olympic event, my mother would have been a gold medalist.

Mom and I sometimes lifted our sagging spirits by going to town to window shop for hats. If we felt brave, we'd go into a store and actually try them on, always worried that the clerks knew our budget was tight, and we weren't there to buy. We tried to keep straight faces, faking our serious interest.

"Do you think this one would be okay with the green suit I'm taking to Chicago?" Mom said with gravity.

"I'm not sure the color is exactly right. We'll have to bring your suit in to see if it's a match," I answered, giving us an honorable escape from the hat shop.

As I readied myself to leave the hospital that first evening, Mom gripped my hand with urgency. "I don't think I'm going to make it," she said. "I want you to see that I'm buried in my favorite red dress. It's hanging in the front bedroom closet." All I could do was nod.

But over the next two weeks, her health improved, and she got stronger. "Hand me that hat box," she said one day. She took the hat out and perched it on the box lid, where she could admire it. "Yes, this hat is definitely me." She stroked the veil.

Several days later, when I left to go home, she promised, "When I get out of the hospital," I'm wearing this hat home."

"I believe it, Mom." I laughed and kissed her goodbye. "Hat power!"

Though I couldn't be there several weeks later when she was discharged, my father assured me that he'd wheeled her out of the hospital in her pajamas and robe wearing the perky red hat perched on her head, with her hugging the hat box on her lap.

My mother eventually went back to her church pew, sporting her new red hat. She lived for many more years. I will always believe it's because she taught me the power of the hat.

These days, due to changing hat customs and living in a windy community, baseball caps are my usual hat wear. But I still think of Mom when I don a new one before a 5K, to put an extra bounce in my stride.

Hope Sunderland is a retired RN, who hung up her bedpan and enema bucket to write. She usually writes what she hopes is humor from the South Texas Gulf Coast. She's been published in *Byline Magazine, New Christian Voices, Gulf Coast Lifestyles, Bedpan Banter, Humorlabs.com, Chicken Soup for the Soul, Christian Communicator, Journal of Nursing Jocularity,* and *TopFive.com.*

The Best Teacher

By Gargi Mehra

On the morning I was to get the results of my final exams, I sprinted to the closet and then threw on my lucky shirt and trousers in a bid to invoke the Gods of Luck—I was scared out of my wits.

As we drove away from the house, I shared my fears with my mother. She listened carefully and then uttered the most significant words I've ever heard in my life, "Don't worry; you've done your best. Now let it go. You are my daughter. If the worst happens, we will take care of it. We will work out what to do. But I have faith in you. I don't think there will be any problem."

The strength of her words boosted my confidence. As she predicted, there was no problem, and my results were good enough to allay my fears that I would never make it in life. From then on, whenever I face a seemingly insurmountable challenge, I recall what she said that day, and it helps alleviate the tension coursing through my body.

Her words echo in my ears even whenever I apply makeup— don't neglect your neck and ears! Her point has always been, if you're going to whiten your face, you should reserve the same special treatment for your surrounding features which remain neglected in traditional cosmetic routines.

From her I learned how to look beautiful without makeup and how I should never trade elegance for glamour. She taught me that putting cosmetics and jewelry on were not the most important things in the world. She took her cues from her mother. My grandmother was naturally pale and although she didn't apply makeup, she poured generous amounts of talcum powder on her face, neck, and ears, thus whitening an already bright visage.

If you want to look your best, she said then and now, wear a dress that inspires confidence in you. Shampoo your hair on the day of a big event, and style your hair the best you can.

Her expertise in minimalistic glamour didn't extend to technology. At the dawn of the Internet era, shortly after I graduated with a degree in Computer Science Engineering, I had the following conversation with her:

Mom: I have seen a wonderful job ad in the paper. They have even given an email address. Should I give it to you?

Me: Yes.

Mom: Okay, write it down, w-w-w-dot—

Me: What? Are you giving me the website address or the email address?

Mom: There's no difference. It's all the same thing.

Me: No, Mom, tell me the one that doesn't start with the w-w-w.

Mom: (after frantically searching) Okay, it is, careers, c-a-r-e-e-r-s—

Me: Yes?

Mom: "A" inside a circle—

Me: What? What is this about *an inside circle*?

Mom: I don't know! That's what's written here; it's a squiggly thing that looks like a circle with an "a" sitting inside it.

Me: Oh god, Mom, that's pronounced "at-the-rate."

From her I learned that an idle mind really is a devil's workshop. Despite being extremely intelligent and having graduated with an honors degree in Mathematics, she stayed home to raise the children. She had only briefly worked a job, but sacrificed any semblance of a career at the altar for her children's happiness. This meant that she had ample free time in which her mind invariably dwelled on things that went wrong. I assume her mind spins circles around the same portentous issues of her past, her future, and especially the thing that keeps her awake at night—the future of her children and grandchildren. This has taught me that if I wasn't working in an office, I might have been driven insane by the power of my thoughts. I would have become bored, restless, and unfulfilled in life. But luckily I'm not, to her credit. She encouraged me to pursue my degree, showing the same faith in me that she did when I was younger.

I also learned the art of sacrifice from my mother. Would I ever give up a promising career to stay home and raise my children? Would I have the patience to handle a child all day long without any help? I think not. In fact, I know I wouldn't.

Maybe in a subtle way, seeing her sacrifice, I learned to stand up for myself, especially when and if someone says something offensive. Why should we always take it lying down?

Why swallow the insults and retorts that hover at the tip of someone else's tongue? Don't others have a responsibility to be polite? Even if I ever did manage to unleash a blistering repartee, I'd feel so overwrought with guilt afterwards that it wouldn't feel worth it.

To be fair, I did absorb the tenets of politeness, humility, and the ability to work hard without shouting from the rooftops about my successes. She taught me the art of making sensible, realistic, and practical decisions—in life as well as at work.

Seeing her always with a book in her hand, I learned to become a bibliophile. Under her guidance, I'd read almost all the books by PG Wodehouse, Arthur Conan Doyle, and Agatha Christie by age thirteen. In her spare time she always read—whether it was a magazine, a novel, or sometimes even a work of nonfiction that aroused her curiosity.

Even my love of writing and the habit of journaling springs from her. I remember at the dawn of every New Year finding a shiny new diary in the house, its dated pages blank and waiting to be filled. In no time her hand would be running over the pages, filling it with memories and thoughts. The first piece of writing I read from her was, "The Conversion Table," an essay about our stay in a foreign country where we always landed up multiplying the rate. She never pursues publication and is content for her writing to remain within the pages of her diary.

She acts as a fierce critic of my work. In my early days of writing short stories, I showed her a completed work I thought was quite good. She dismissed it immediately, saying she didn't understand the main character's motivations. I stalked off, annoyed at this rebuff, but later when I reread my story, I discovered that she was right, as usual.

When I studied in engineering college, I stayed in the hostel. Oftentimes the lack of supportive friends and the open hostility led me to depression. I would share my feelings with her on the phone whenever she called. She would offer her customary words of encouragement, but her verbal-boost would then be followed up by pages of handwritten letters that she sent to me at the hostel address.

These weren't letters written on numbered diary pages. The stationery she used was a flowery writing pad, yellow pages with lilies and daisies etched in the four corners. Her writing was the same as it had been years ago, the letters long and straight, but nevertheless artistic.

Those letters now reside in the top drawer of my writing desk. Occasionally I take them out, and when I read them, it brings tears to my eyes. Both for the love and support shining through her words and also for the fleeting thought that passes through my mind—will I ever be as good a mother as she is?

I know that answer. Of course I will—I learned from her.

Gargi Mehra is a software professional by day, a writer by night, and a mother at all times. She writes fiction and humor in an effort to unite the two sides of the brain in cerebral harmony. Her work has appeared in numerous literary magazines. Visit her at gargimehra. wordpress.com.

Carousel Time

By m.nicole.r.wildhood

"You don't really understand human nature unless you know why a child on a merry-go-round will wave at his parents every time around and why his parents will always wave back."

—William D. Tammeus

Lesson Number One: Listen Carefully

"Hey, I'm late." My sister shouts from the living room. "Can you toss down my purse?" She races around gathering gloves, boots, and coat. "Oh, and my scarf?"

"It's like seventy degrees outside!" I shout from my room.

"Will you just do it?" she says frantically.

"Yeah," my brother says. "And while you're at it, my Rockies hat is on my bedpost. Could you toss that down, too!"

I'm the oldest of three, but my room was in the middle on the second floor overlooking the living room from the balcony. Apparently, this meant that I had equal access to both siblings' stuff.

I sigh and roll my eyes. "Fine, but I'll be tossing my laundry over, too, so watch out."

"Seriously?" My sister groans.

"It'll be just like that time we shoved all those balloons off the balcony for Dad's surprise birthday party!" I shout from my closet.

We got used to tossing things—and requests—over the balcony. The Christmas Day spread in the first-floor living room was best captured from a camera balanced on the balcony's railing. Shouting over it was more effective than the "intercom" system my parents tried to set up in each of our rooms. Now, it was easier to hear the dinner bell—it probably was an actual Christmas tree ornament at one point—than Mom's vocal cords during the meal roundup call. But when someone was in trouble, no measure of happy, angel-getting-its-wings jingling would suffice. Mom would discover a broken flower vase, or mud on the carpet, or a bad report card, and the need for a specific kid to answer for the mess would be signaled.

And this is how Mom taught me that "Megan" and "David" sound nearly identical. Now, *of course*, it was *always* my brother who was being summoned. But even if I wasn't behind the closed door of my childhood bedroom with headphones on studying, I was still always startled at the name David. Every single time.

Lesson Number Two: Care About Your Pain

"Stop rubbing your face," Mom said, interrupting Dad's recounting of his workday. I didn't bother to explain that my acne felt like mosquito bites and that the hot shame of being called out in front of my porcelain-faced siblings wouldn't help things.

"Harassing your face is how you get scars," Mom persisted, shooting an apologetic look at Dad, who smiled and kept chattering.

"Doesn't just apply to my face," I whispered into my glass of water, as I finished dinner in silence and stomped off to my room.

A couple hours later, Mom knocked on my door.

"Good night," she said before I could open it. "Did you wash your face?"

"Yes," I huffed and sunk back down under my music.

"You're sure? That cream and cleanser were expensive," she said.

"Yes, as was the intelligence-insulting training you made me sit through on how to use them," I shouted, not bothering to turn down my music. *Does she even want me to like her?*

I thought I heard my bedroom, and then my bathroom door, open and close in rapid succession, so I tore my headphones off and stood up fast enough to flip over my desk chair. *Does my sister have a better face than me?* I was getting ready to say if I encountered her in my room. *Am I not pretty enough to fit in?*

"As if I care," I said. "I'm a band geek!" I looked around and verified that I was alone. Then I freed the tears billowing behind my eyelids. I didn't think the acne battle was one a hormonal, oily-skinned teenager, such as myself, could win, so despite how much the infections sometimes hurt, there was nothing I could do.

"I don't know why you feel like lying to me is a good idea," Mom said, after the dishes were done the next night.

"I don't know why you feel like lying to *me* is a good idea." I sneered.

"Lying about what?" Mom planted fists on hips and feet hip width apart. "So I suppose you know what about then," she said irritatingly calmly.

"Does it matter?"

"When was the last time you washed your face?"

"When was the last time you asked me if I washed my face?"

"The same night that your sink was dry, two minutes after you told me you had washed your face."

"What is your obsession with my face?" I shouted. "Is it that I don't look enough like you? Is it that I'm ugly? What is so bothersome about me that you would invade my personal space to check up on me?" I didn't wait for an answer. I stayed in my room the rest of the night until I thought my parents were asleep.

As I skulked past their room to the stairs to find a midnight snack, I thought I heard Mom sniffle and say, "I just wish she was motivated by love." I never told her that I heard her, but I started letting her feel my sink, wet with water I'd used to soothe my face. Every single time.

Lesson Number Three: Every Test is a Game

"These games," Mom said, pulling a colorful cardboard box from her pack, "need to learn how to be played." She spread out construction paper, Styrofoam shapes, paper cups, and bags of sequins around the table.

"Okay," I said, grabbing all the bright, crisp shapes. "Clearly, they need to be stacked by color." I instructed my six-year-old sister. She shook her head.

"No!" she said, straining across the table and nabbing as many shapes as she could. She started arranging them into configurations I couldn't identify, until she declared, "Flowers!" My two-year-old brother took the shapes within his reach, piled them messily, and then smashed them repeatedly.

"No!" I said, throwing my hands up. "Stacked by color, then by size." I tried not to tear up. "You take all the green shapes, and then you take all the green circles and put them at the bottom, then all the green squares, and then all the green triangles," I repeated, louder and louder over my brother's and then my sister's tears.

"This is not a test," Mom said, putting her hands over my hands, clutching a green triangle and a red square. "This is not a test." My siblings left the table to go play with their own toys, but Mom had solitary games that needed to be taught how to be played, which I found even more fun since I could actually follow the rules without impediment. Of course, the only way I could permit myself to truly enjoy them was Mom's constant reassurance, "This is not a test." I did math problems in ways I hadn't learned in school; I read in a mirror; I drew pictures of my favorite animals with my eyes closed. I would learn many years later that, technically, they *were* tests. Mom was a Special Ed teacher at the elementary level for twenty-seven years, and was researching potential curriculum being developed to support learning-challenged children.

I took the SATs my junior year of high school so that if I needed to take them again, I would have time. The analogies were fun and the reading comprehension was engaging, so I had a hard stumble when the spatial reasoning section paraded out from nowhere. The two-dimensional figures refused to be categorized; the drawings would not be stacked. Word problems had been my sanctuary in math and math-like territory; here, the chaos of unfamiliar arrangements threatened to tie a chain around my erstwhile, high-score's neck and drown it, sinking my college prospects and career aspirations, and any hope of a meaningful life right along with it.

My scantron blurred, and a tear blotted some of my answers—ones that I was pretty confident were right. And then I heard Mom whisper, "This is not a test." She placed a red circle over the stick-figure on my test booklet. I blinked and looked at the problem and repeated her words every single time, right until the end.

Lesson Number Four: Grace is Golden

"Be back in half an hour," I said, rustling my purse for my keys.

"Worst. Place. Ever to pause this movie!" My friend laughed and groaned.

"Really? I haven't seen it." I upturned my purse on the couch.

"Well, just hurry. Okay?" Jess tossed my keys to me from the coffee table.

"You couldn't have found them just a *bit* sooner?" I said, glaring at my mess of purse contents.

Jess held my purse near the end of the sofa cushion, and I swept my belongings back into it. I shoved my arms into my coat as I ran out the door to my gold minivan waiting at the edge of her driveway. I noted the clock as I started the engine: 11:47 p.m. *I'd be home in time to turn off the curfew clock if I don't hit any red lights.*

"I just barely made it," I said, back at Jess's house for the rest of the movie.

"We really ought to come up with a better way around this whole racing back and forth thing," Jess said, peering over my shoulder. "Nice parking job."

One tire was up on the curb, almost touching the grass of her front lawn. "I guess I forgot I wasn't in a hurry anymore."

"Well, good thing it's dark out. Otherwise, your car would be shining like a beacon announcing your mistake!" She closed the door after me and waited for me to take off my shoes.

"Yeah, I don't know what I was thinking choosing gold for the new color."

"Do you really think *any* color would have made it better than your parents gave you a minivan to drive to high school?"

"On the bright side, I can fit the entire alto saxophone section in my car, which cuts down on time spent organizing rides." I handed Jess three remotes and shrugged as she took them, swiftly hitting a combination of buttons on each of them and unfreezing Morgan Freeman's face to say, "Geology is the study of pressure and time."

I might say the same about motherhood, at least from the receiving end. I hadn't been allowed to watch *The Shawshank Redemption,* which is half the reason I snuck out to Jess's to watch it. The other half was principle; curfew is an easy rule to break safely. I explained this to my parents while I was in the beginning stages of planning my wedding, which wasn't quite ten years after the fact, but some other rules, like my dad's "Ten-Year Immunity" one, could be fudged a little, too.

"Oh, we knew you took the Golden Egg out after midnight," Mom said during a phone call we'd scheduled for wedding planning.

"Every single time?" I said, trying to hide my shock that she wouldn't have confronted me about disobeying the rules.

"Every single time."

m.nicole.r.wildhood is a Colorado native living in Seattle—and missing the sun—since 2006. She has been a saxophone player and registered scuba diver for over half her life. In addition to blogging, she writes poetry, fiction, and short nonfiction, which have appeared in *The Sun, Lodestone, Ballard: A Journal of Street Poetry*, and *Café Aphra*. She and her husband, a gifted structural engineer and artist, often collaborate on poetry and painting pieces. She is an advocate for those experiencing mental and emotional suffering, and celebrates the misfits, the non-conventional, and the bold. Visit her at megan. thewildhoods.com.

It's Okay to Be a Bitch

By Lisa Webb

I thought my mother was awful when I was a teenager. I think entire years went by where we didn't get along. I thought she was the meanest mom in the world.

Why did I always have to be the one who couldn't stay out late? Why did she always need to know where I was going? When I went on performance trips with my dance group, why did she have to be the mom who volunteered to come along as a chaperone? I was positive that my mom's main goal in life was to make sure I didn't have any fun. Not even a little.

But I was determined. I would find a way to have the kind of fun I wanted; even if it meant tearing through the tranquility of our home like a teenage hurricane.

One Thursday evening, I left my house in jeans and a T-shirt, with the world's smallest, and most sparkly, tube top underneath, and a matching teeny tiny skirt rolled up in my hand bag. I was ready to hit the bar with my fake ID, drink copious amounts of alcohol, and most likely follow that up with some poor decision making.

I was in that magic time in life where I was nearly finished high school and waiting for my next chapter to begin. It was my final semester and I only needed a few more credits to graduate, which meant that I only needed to be in school a few hours a day, leaving me with far too much free time and the ability to sleep in at my leisure. Every day became the weekend. (The fact that my parents worked in the morning—and that I lived under their roof—didn't cross my adolescent mind.)

When I stumbled out of the smoky bar at 2:00 a.m., giggling with my girlfriends, we quickly saw that the chances of us getting a taxi home weren't looking good. There were too many drunken twenty-somethings and not enough cabs. That was always the way. We spotted a few guys from our high school that lived in our neighborhood and we all decided that we'd just stagger home together. We didn't take into account that we lived clear across the city, and it would probably take us a several hours to walk home at the pace we were going. When you're eighteen and hopped up on vodka coolers, small details like this can easily slip the mind.

By 3:30 a.m. we had made pretty good progress. We were more than halfway home when my cousin Ashley, who was also my best friend and lived down the street, grabbed my arm and pointed down the road.

"Oh no, is that your van?" she was pointing at the 1986 station wagon minivan with wood paneling down the side that was driving towards us, lights shining bright.

I stood like a deer in the headlights. There was only one van in town that could possibly be that old and embarrassing, and my parents drove it.

"Yup, that's totally your van." Ashley confirmed, as she joined me in disbelief. "You're screwed," were her last words to me before my mom pulled up in the minivan, rolled down the window, and exposed her bedhead, giant red bathrobe, and flannel pajamas underneath.

"Lisa, you get in this vehicle right now." Mom spat the words with a rage in her voice that can only be brought out by trolling the neighborhood for her underage daughter at 3:30 a.m. on a work night.

"That sucks," Ashley muttered under her breath as I made my way to the van, my shoes in my hand and feet covered in dirt.

"Ashley! You too!" The fire in my mom's eyes let my cousin know this was not the hour to be messing with her aunt.

Too embarrassed to even make eye contact with the boys from school, we climbed into the back of the van, stoic from the vodka coolers. We were more embarrassed about being picked up by the woody-wagon than we were worried about the aftermath of punishment that would follow.

The later teen years were a difficult period in our house. I was still living at home, but was adult enough to know that there were only so many things my parents could do to punish me anymore. The power struggle of adolescence was coming to an end. The years of shouting and slamming doors were nearly over. We were coming out of the fog, yet we were still unable to see the road ahead.

There were a lot of bullets dodged in our house during those adolescent years. No hospital visits, no criminal records, no teenage pregnancies. I even came out on the other side with a few university degrees, a husband, and a couple of kids. In that order to boot! I guess my mom didn't do too badly of a job raising me after all.

It's been a decade and a half since that night I got picked up in the woody-wagon, and I now have two daughters of my own that I worry about daily. Life is funny like that, isn't it?

In fifteen more years, will I find myself slowly driving through the neighborhood at an ungodly hour, ready to kidnap my daughter from her pack of friends? Will I threaten to phone the bar and tell them about the fake ID that I know she has, but I can't prove? Will I ground her from her first boyfriend and take away her phone? I haven't a clue.

What I do know is that my mom wasn't being as awful as I thought she was. She loved me, and was doing everything she could to keep me safe and out of trouble. My mom didn't try to be my best friend; I already had one of those. She was being my mother: firm, tough, loving—and if she needed to be, a bitch. Because when it came to keeping her slightly wild teenager on the straight and narrow, sometimes she had to be just that.

She spent years being the woman that I now need to be for my daughters. And today, she's my best friend. She watches me raise my daughters, and gives me a sympathetic, knowing smile when I tell her that it's tough.

"Oh, you think this is tough now?" she says. "You just wait until they're eighteen."

Lisa Webb is the author behind the blog, *Canadian Expat Mom*. She lives in the South of France with her husband and their two French-born daughters. When her family isn't in the land of wine and cheese, they can be found exploring the globe with far too much luggage. Lisa is currently working on her first novel; a humorous memoir about her adventures in France. You can also find her on *The Huffington Post* and *BLUNTmoms*.

The Gift of Language

By Olga Mecking

My mother gave me many gifts. For example, there was the caterpillar that she had single-handedly assembled for me even though she is not at all a crafty person. Years later, I still have that caterpillar in one of the drawers at my parents' place. She also taught me many things: that doing what you love is important; that you need to work hard to achieve your goals; that independence is a crucial part of happiness.

But the one gift and the one lesson I will always be grateful for is the gift of languages. My mother is a highly educated, wise woman. She speaks Polish, German, French, and some Dutch. But English is like a second mother tongue to her.

When I was little, I had a little English at the Polish kindergarten I attended. They taught me a few words, but it was nowhere near enough. My mother was dismayed when she found out that the only thing I knew were the names of colors, and she decided to take matters into her own hands.

She bought an exercise book and had me fill it in, day after day. Once I had a very basic understanding of English grammar, she asked me to read aloud to her. She chose a book I loved and knew almost by heart in Polish, "Winnie the Pooh" by A.A. Milne.

Reading aloud was hard at first. I thought the English language was crazy. I mean, why did the past tense never even remotely resemble the present tense of the same word? How was I supposed to know that "ate" was the same as "eat" or that there are so many ways to pronounce "th"? I didn't understand a lot of what I was reading and the experience was extremely frustrating. I had to stop every few words and ask, "What does this mean?" or "How do you pronounce that?" I was very close to quitting. My mother would have none of that, though.

With her encouragement, I read on, word after word, sentence after sentence. With time and the help of the exercise book, I struggled through "Winnie the Pooh", slowly, frustratingly.

I don't know when or even why, but suddenly everything started to make sense. It was like a switch went from "English off" to "English on." The weird sounds started to come together to create clear, perfectly understandable words, which in turn morphed into comprehensive sentences and after that, into the story that I knew so well in another language.

We finished "Winnie the Pooh" and moved on to "A House at Pooh's Corner." I started to enjoy the experience, especially the bonding time I had with my mom. We read many more books after that, until I was able to read them on my own.

Later, I also had English classes at my school and The British Council. But it was my mother who had shown me the importance and the beauty of this language. We would even speak English together and it became our own private tongue.

Even though I was quickly becoming proficient, my mother was always there to give support, or provide me with new books to read. Before I knew it, learning English went from being a chore, something that needed to be done, to being fun and exciting.

I worked hard at my classes, not only because I had to prepare for exams, but also because I wanted to speak perfect English. I knew that it was an important language. And again, it was my own hard-working mother who showed me how to face challenges and not quit when problems appeared. Even though I could read the books rather well, I still had a lot to work on. Tenses were my weak point. I simply couldn't understand why one had to differentiate between "something has been done" and "something was done," for example.

Again, my mother came to the rescue. When you ask native speakers why they say things a certain way, they'd answer, "Oh, that's just how our language works", which is great but not helpful. My mother couldn't answer many of my grammar-related questions, but together we found a great book that explained all the many tenses and gave examples. It was a huge help.

With time, I could tackle these challenges myself or ask my teachers. And I became truly proficient in English. Now, I have no problems whatsoever writing in this language. On the contrary, I love it. I discovered the beauty of English and now use it more than ever.

I'm still not perfect. When I speak English, my accent leaves a lot to be desired. I wish I'd somehow absorbed my mother's perfect Boston accent but no matter how hard I try, I can't seem to make it work. Additionally, I've come across so many dialects and versions of this language that my English is a combination of all of them. However, I have hopes that watching *Outlander* will add a little Scottish accent to this mix. Jokes aside, for me English is so much more than just a language. Being able to speak, read, and write in this tongue is the source of great pride. But at the same time, it is something my mother and I share together.

Through her I found a passion for a language that she speaks so well. I worked hard to learn it and my struggles paid off in a way I wouldn't have thought possible. It's all thanks to her.

Now I have children on my own, and I'm raising them to speak three languages: my native Polish, German (the language of the country my husband comes from), and Dutch (as we live in the Netherlands).

My eldest goes to an international school and brings home English words, songs, and phrases. I smile when I hear her speak it. She doesn't have classes in this language, but picks it up from other children. But when the time comes, I will give her the gift of the English language. I think I know the perfect book to start.

Olga Mecking is a Polish woman living in the Netherlands with her German husband and three trilingual children. She is a translator, blogger, and writer. Her blog, *The European Mama*, is all about life abroad, raising children, and traveling. She also is a regular contributor to *World Moms Blog, BLUNTmoms,* and *Multicultural Kid Blogs.* Her writings have been published on *Scary Mommy, Mamalode,* and *The Huffington Post.* When not blogging or thinking about blogging, she can be found reading books, drinking tea, or cooking.

A Breath of Wise Words

By Joy Hedding

This too shall pass.

Those words I hear in my head anytime something is too funny, too serious, too overwhelming, too special, or simply too much. "This too shall pass." Wiser words have never been given breath.

I first recall my mom saying those words to me in middle school. I vividly remember hearing that phrase after being devastated by some middle-school girl drama. Bawling and carrying on as only a thirteen-year-old girl could do, my mom comforted me with that phrase.

In high school, when I felt like I was drowning in all the cheerleading, pom-pom, marching band, drama, and science fair minutia, she would say, "This too shall pass." While away at college, and figuring out how to change my major and stay afloat when I was so far out of my league, I would call home upset, "This too, shall pass." While my husband and I were arguing over where to live after college graduation, my mom reminded me, "This too shall pass." When I was in labor with my first baby, "Hold on, this too shall pass." And when my husband was on life support and I was at my deepest, darkest moments, she held my hand and prayed with me, "This too shall pass."

The lessons I've learned from my mother over the years are too numerous to even list. Of all of them, "This too shall pass," is one of the most important. Growing up is tough. Having her voice in my head saying her favorite phrase carried me through many rotten moments; the days when the popular girls weren't nice; the days when I wasn't nice, and then felt guilty about what I'd done.

I heard her voice in my head when I received letters of reward and rejection. When struggling with decisions that at the time seemed to be life or death, could result in success or failure, or so important I couldn't keep my wits about me, there was always this whisper of calm, "This too shall pass." Knowing there was always some sort of light at the end of the tunnel made all things bearable.

One of the most important lessons she taught me with this particular phrase is that *all* things pass. The good, the bad, the beautiful, and the less than desirable—they all pass.

She taught me to enjoy the life happening right in front of me, because it will pass on, and one day I'll find my house as tidy as I'd like it, all the things in their places, the floors clean, and the beds made. She reminds me that we will one day become empty nesters with a quiet house longing for the craziness that we now have; that this insane time in my life, *the right now* with four children under my roof, chaos around every corner, and crumbs in every nook and cranny, will pass. It will be over in the blink of an eye. And I'll miss it. She reminds me to enjoy this time because, "This too shall pass."

Another lesson I've learned from this amazing woman is to "make a list and get stuff done." Even now, when she comes to visit, she has me make a list of the errands that need to get done. I'm nearly forty years old, and I still do as I'm told. I list all the things I've needed to accomplish, but never quite found the time to finish, tell my mom what's on the list, load up the truck, and off we go. More often than not, I'm willing to quit before the list is complete. She says, "Drive through and get us some coffee so we can get this all done today. Then tomorrow we can just sit and enjoy our time." She cracks the whip, I'm telling you. *Cracks.The.Whip.* But man, she gets things done. And she knows how good it feels to get those things done. She's taught me to plow through and keep trucking on.

While she was raising me, she didn't lose herself in being just a mom. I witnessed her foster the friendships she held dear and sat through countless coffee dates. I'd grab a book and read, while she and her bestie chatted up the morning at a local diner. I didn't really participate in these coffee dates unless reading every *Nancy Drew* book ever written counts.

Then one day as a teenager I started to listen and contribute here and there. As a mom myself, I now know how special it was to be included in these times with my mom and her friends. They taught me the value of friendship, the art of conversation, and the simple pleasure of time spent with good friends. "Be a good friend," is one lesson she shared with me, for which I'm forever grateful.

My mom also has these quirky things she says. "Caddywhompus" is one of them. I didn't realize this word wasn't common until I went away to school. And wow—use that word once in a place where you are already considered to speak too quickly and have an accent, and you can silence a room, repeat yourself, and suddenly have a stand-up routine going.

There's another word she likes—a lot. It's shoot, but not *shoot*. It's the other one. You know—the *shit* one. I've rarely heard my mother swear in my time on this earth, but when I have, you can guarantee I heard the other *shoot*.

She also sings, "Whoops-a-doodle-a-dandy-dee!" Singing this song is her way to wake up a sleeping child, deal with moments when she would have used foul language, or just lighten the mood. When my childhood friends and I reminisce about the old days, one of them always brings up my mom coming in the morning after a sleepover singing loudly, "Whoops-a-doodle-a-dandy-dee!" over and over until we started moving.

My mom taught me so much. I'm still learning from her. I hope I have my ears, eyes, and heart open to learn all I can while we still have time together. I dream of being able to pass on as much knowledge about being a good person to my children as she has to me. I'm thankful for each and every lesson she's taught me and wonder what the next one will be.

Oh—the next time you want to swear like a sailor, smile instead and remember, "This too shall pass." Then let out a "WHOOPS-A-DOODLE-A-DANDY-DEE!" and be on your merry way!

Joy Hedding, aka Evil Joy, is wife to one Dr. Evil and mom to four children she lovingly refers to as spawn. Often funny, always honest, and occasionally serious, Joy writes about life as she sees it. She's passionate about her family, snowboarding, running, blogging, and reading.

Twenty-Four Signs You Are Becoming Your Mother

By Sarah Cottrell

I swore up and down (and left and right) that when I had kids I would never be like my mother. Nope. I would be the cool mom who did yoga with her kids and never yelled. I would bring my kids on fun spontaneous excursions just because. The living room walls could be drawn on—with washable crayons, of course—while the sound of French language tapes enriching my children played in the background.

And then I had kids.

My walls are indeed coated in a film of Crayola, which while called "washable," did not in fact wash off. Those language tapes were fun for seven minutes before the kids started crying that they wanted to watch *Curious George* instead. Fun spontaneous excursions became emergency trips to the Starbucks drive-thru—or the liquor store.

I was so sure I was still a cool mom until one day when I faked a headache to get the kids to quiet down for a while. If that gem can work on my husband then it might help me win some sympathy points with the wee ones. Then I wondered why this tactic seemed so familiar. And that is when I realized—I am becoming my mother!

Here are twenty-four signs that you, too, are becoming your mother:

1. No child leaves your house without suffering the mom test: sniffing for weird smells, checking hands and faces for dirt, and asking eighteen questions about possibly having to pee, poop, or needing a snack.
2. You complain about being bloated, having backaches, needing more coffee, or being tired.
3. You wear mom pants of the yoga or sweat or elastic band jean variety.
4. Before leaving the house you say cryptic things like, "I need to put my face on." And then you rush to slap on some mascara.
5. You once got busted tweezing a rogue black chin hair guided by your reflection in the stainless steel toaster.
6. You mutter under your breath so much that your own voice has become the constant white noise of your day.
7. You have started numerous lectures with the sentence, "When I was your age ..."
8. You have worn a coat over your pajamas, at the great embarrassment of your kids, for morning drop off.
9. You sing loudly in the car and wax poetic about music from the 1980s.
10. You have mastered the never-ending goodbye by starting new conversations in mid-sentence.

11. Everyone in your house knows when you have eaten ice cream because with middle mom age comes lactose intolerance.

12. When fashionable means rips, graphics, distressed fabric, or questionable hemlines on your children's clothing, you have been known to suddenly become super conservative.

13. You say things like, one, two, ... OMG! Don't make me say three!

14. You have mastered your mother's slightly-evil-mostly-disapproving mom glare. So much so that your glare works on the neighborhood kids with as much punch as it does on your own children.

15. The PTA is a really exciting place to be.

16. After a few years of parenthood, you have finally realized that that wasn't coffee in your mom's mug at every sporting/recital/birthday party.

17. You lie so much to your children about food, reasons why you can't (fill in the blank), and reasons why you have to (fill in the blank), that you are starting to believe that spaghetti really is hair from a giant evil ninja and that if you eat it all you really might win the Golden Sword of All Knowing.

18. You can't help but over share details about your children, like that time your son mooned the Brownie troop or how cute his tushie is.

19. It turns out that moms fart with reckless abandon. Especially after ice cream (see #11).

20. The excuse "Because I gave birth to you" is really handy.

21. Your kids are deeply embarrassed by your workout outfit and the fact that you do Pilates in the living room to DVDs. Hello, Jane Fonda!

22. You once told your daughter that you hope she has children just like her. Pfft, that'll teach her.
23. You now need half a pot of coffee to be functional in the morning. And then half a bottle of wine twelve hours later.
24. You now have very strong opinions on Spanx, diets, and the appropriate number of years that you can still wear maternity pants after you've birthed your last child.

Say what you will, the day will come when you sneak an extra slice of cake and start muttering about starting a diet tomorrow. Right then and there, BOOM it will hit you—you are indeed becoming your mother. And while this fact in and of itself is not the end of the world, it is the final calling card from the universe that motherhood is not a job for the weak of will or heart.

The truth is, discovering that you are becoming your mother means that you are doing something right. And if all else fails, it can at the very least mean that you finally understand why your mother was so crazy.

Congratulations, you've come full circle.

Sarah Cottrell lives in Maine with her boat-builder husband and two loud boys. She blogs at the *Bangor Daily News* under the name *Housewife Plus*. In 2012, Sarah earned her MFA and since then she has been featured on *BlogHer*, *In the Powder Room*, *Mamalode*, *Mamapedia*, *Scary Mommy*, and more.

A Note from the Editor

Thank you for reading Only Trollops Shave Above the Knee. We invite you to visit our individual blogs and connect with us on social media. Each writer in this book can be found on networks like Facebook, Goodreads, Twitter, Instagram, Pinterest, and more. You can find the links on the book's landing page at:

www.bluelobsterbookco.com/onlytrollopsshaveabovetheknee

We sincerely hope that you enjoyed our crazy and endearing stories. If you did like the book, please share the good news with all of your friends, family, co-workers, and anyone who has ever been birthed by a mother. When you're done spreading the word, could you also leave us a review on Amazon? It only takes a minute or two and really helps increase the visibility of the book. We sincerely appreciate the feedback!

Is it time to find something else to read? If you loved Only Trollops Shave Above the Knee, then you might enjoy Blue

Lobster Book Co.'s original publications The Mother of All Meltdowns and Clash of the Couples. Both are available on Amazon, Apple Store, and B&N.com.

Thanks again for all of your support!

Crystal Ponti

Made in the USA
Middletown, DE
12 May 2015